THE ⟨
OF MATTHEW

"...a positive and practical way to change the heart of any worshiping community that truly desires to read the Scriptures afresh."
Earl S. Johnson, Jr., Pastor, First Presbyterian Church, Johnstown, NY

"...a landmark in biblical exegesis."
Christopher Rowland, Dean Ireland's Professor of Exegesis of Holy Scripture, Queen's College, Oxford

"...an ambitious program for group study of seminal passages from Matthew."
Edgar V. McKnight, Research Professor and William R. Kenan Jr., Professor of Religion Emeritus, Furman University

"...a sure guide for leading to an open awareness of our own contextual approach to exegesis."
J. Severino Croatto, Department of Biblical Studies, Instituto Universitario ISEDET, Buenos Aires

"Invites participants into respectful sharing and deeper understanding of the Bible as Scripture."
K.C. Ptomey, Jr., Pastor, Westminster Presbyterian Church, Nashville, TN

"...makes me re-cognize again and again the inevitability and the importance of interpretive choices."
Tat-siong Benny Liew, Associate Professor of New Testament, Chicago Theological Seminary

"...provides a practicable model for disciplined study and group discussion."
Kang Na, Assistant Professor of Religion, Westminster College New Wilmington, PA

"Daniel Patte con Stubbs, Ukpong Y Velunta nos ofrecen un excelente quia metodologica, clara, sencilla y al mismo tiempo de notable seriedad academica."
Else Tamez, Universidad Biblica Lainoamericana

The Gospel of Matthew

A Contextual Introduction
for Group Study

Daniel Patte

with
Monya A. Stubbs, Justin Ukpong, and
Revelation E. Velunta

Abingdon Press
Nashville

THE GOSPEL OF MATTHEW:
A CONTEXTUAL INTRODUCTION FOR GROUP STUDY

Copyright © 2003 by Abingdon Press

This book is printed on acid-free paper.

Library of Congress Cataloging-in-Publication Data

Patte, Daniel.
    The Gospel of Matthew : a contextual introduction for group study / Daniel Patte with Monya A. Stubbs, Justin Ukpong, and Revelation E. Velunta.
        p. cm.
Includes bibliographical references.
    ISBN 0-687-02214-2 (pbk.)
    1. Bible. N.T. Matthew—Introduuction. I. Title.

BS2575.52.P38 2003
226.2'0071—dc21

                                                        2003005564

The logo on the cover skillfully represents the three moments of any interpretation of a scriptural text:
  a) the reader encounters the power of the text and seizes a significant teaching for believers–see the textual whirlwind in the center;
  b) the reader discovers the wealth of teaching offered by the text in the roundtable context of reading--see the people joining hands; and
  c) the reader assesses the choice of interpretation for a particular religious and ethical context–see the bread and chalice and the face-to-face encounter.

03 04 05 06 07 08 09 10 11 12 — 10 9 8 7 6 5 4 3 2 1

MANUFACTURED IN THE UNITED STATES OF AMERICA

Contents

Introduction

This short book provides an introduction to the Gospel of Matthew for Bible study groups. The contextual approach used here is appropriate and useful for undergraduate colleges, seminary New Testament classes, and adult Bible study groups. The book is aimed at helping members of such groups to:

1. Identify the wealth of teachings offered by selected passages of Matthew for believers in diverse life contexts;
2. Gain a critical perspective on interpretations of the Bible, which they encounter in present-day cultural and religious contexts; and
3. Assume responsibility for their choice of a biblical teaching and for the way their beliefs about the Bible affect other people.

For these purposes, this book invites you as a member of the study group to participate in three roundtable discussions on each Bible passage:

Roundtable 1: Share with the group what you consider to be the primary teaching for Christian believers of each passage of Matthew, and appreciate contributions by the other members of the group for their insights about the text;

Roundtable 2: Make a critical comparison of the group's interpretations with published interpretations originating in different cultural contexts, taking note of the different interpretive choices involved in scholarly commentaries, sermons, artistic interpretations (in literature and in visual arts), and their own interpretations; and

Roundtable 3: Discuss and assess the relative value of each interpretation for believers and for their neighbors in particular contexts.

This book first focuses on three important passages in the Gospel of Matthew: the Beatitudes (Matt. 5:3-12) as part of the Sermon on the Mount in chapters 1-3 of this book; the encounter of Jesus and the Canaanite woman (Matt. 15:21-28) in chapter 4; and the Great Commission (Matt.

28:16-20) in chapter 5. Discussion of these passages leads to a consideration of many aspects of the Gospel of Matthew. Chapter 6 considers Matthew as a whole and presents important issues for interpreting this Gospel today.

Participation in a Bible Study Group

This emphasis on participation in a study group reflects the experience of teachers in various contexts around the world. Adults learn best in groups, in which they learn from one another. In this technological age, roundtables can be virtual, by meeting in a chat room, as well as physical, by actually sitting around a table, or a combination of both. In all cases, conversation with others makes it much easier to gain a critical perspective on a biblical book and its interpretations.

In the first roundtable, the sharing of different interpretations with others opens the rich treasures of the text and allows each participant to see the strengths and limitations of her or his own interpretation. This roundtable sets the tone and prepares the way for the rest of the roundtable discussions.

The second roundtable welcomes additional conversation partners. Who will they be? Many people are ready to share their interpretations— they publish them. Members of the group will be invited to read some of these. But conversations with these authors can only be indirect and one-way at best. The second roundtable also provides each member of the group with live conversation partners, who together can compare their respective assessments of these published interpretations, and, in the process, refine each of their own interpretations.

The third roundtable invites the group to assess each interpretation, including your own, by relating it to life and particular situations. How does each interpretation affect Christian believers and their neighbors in this life context? You can then recognize that the choice of an interpretation has far-reaching consequences because believers "live by" Scripture and their interpretations of it.

Each roundtable involves three moments: preparation, discussion, and sharing results.

Preparation of the Roundtable. The better prepared the group members are, the more valuable the learning experience for each roundtable participant. You have a responsibility toward the other participants of the group—be it a class or some other Bible study group. You should come ready to contribute to the discussion to ensure that it will be a rich learning experience for all.

This book is designed to help you prepare for each roundtable discussion. It is an invitation to discuss. For the first roundtable, the book provides discussion starters that have been found particularly fruitful. For the second roundtable, the book adds fuel to the discussion by presenting existing published interpretations that have been formatted for easy incorporation into group discussion. One of the distinctive features of this book is the presentation of these interpretations in a way that allows ready comparison of published interpretations with those prepared by members of the group. For the third roundtable, the book provides questions to help you assess the relative values of all the interpretations previously discussed by asking members of the group to consider how believers would "live by" each of these interpretations of the scriptural text in a given life context.

Roundtable Discussion. To make sure that all the members are able to contribute to the discussion, the roundtable groups should be relatively small and hold to a clearly defined schedule. A large Bible study group or class is best subdivided in small groups of from six to ten people. The best size for a group varies with the time available for the roundtable. A good rule of thumb is that each participant needs at least five minutes. Thus, roundtable groups of six are ideal for thirty-minute discussions. Members should remain in the same group for each set of three roundtable discussions.

Sharing Results. Preparing to share the results of the discussion with the larger group helps make the discussion more fruitful by giving it a clear objective. Thus, even small Bible study groups that are not subdivided should prepare a summary of results. In a larger group, the results of the roundtable discussions are shared in plenary sessions.

The first set of three roundtables may require three full sessions because participants need time to get to know one another and have extended time for the plenaries. Afterward, a set of three roundtables on each Bible passage can normally be held during the same session time. In any case, you should be prepared for all three roundtables before the subsequent sessions.

A Contextual Approach Fostering Active Participation in Bible Study Group

Stereotypically, groups tend to include two types of participants: the talkers, who fail to listen, and the listeners, who fail to talk. A contextual approach provides a leveled field on which all are in a position to contribute actively to the discussion.

A few members of a Bible study group—specifically, the talkers—may feel they have a lot to contribute. They regularly read the Bible, and they are convinced that they grasp right away the meaning of each biblical text. Participating in a Bible study group will be the occasion for sharing their knowledge of the Bible and what it means. In this case, the problem is not only that they silence other members of the group, preventing them from participating in the discussion, but also and primarily that they demonstrate their belief that they have nothing to learn from other members of the group. Worse still, they may believe that they have nothing to learn from the biblical text—since they already know what it means. This denies that the biblical text is Scripture, that it is a book for believers to live by, meaning that the Bible truly plays its role when it confronts, challenges, addresses, transforms, or affirms the believers' daily lives. A contextual approach deliberately accounts for this role of the biblical text as Scripture to live by. Thus, this book invites "talkers" to become listeners, to become aware of the contextual and scriptural character of their own interpretations, and thus to recognize that other contexts call for quite different interpretations.

Other members of a group—the listeners—may feel intimidated by the prospect of actively participating in such Bible study groups. They fear, initially at least, that they will not have anything to contribute to the discussion. Since they believe their knowledge of the biblical text is limited, should they not begin by listening to those who know more about it? After all, they have come to learn about the Bible. The contextual approach in this book is designed to help them overcome this fear. This uneasiness is also a symptom of a much broader problem that needs to be addressed in academic and church circles today; many people, including Christian believers, do not know the Bible.

The fear that one will not have anything valuable to contribute to a Bible study group comes from the feeling that one's interpretation of the Bible will be wrong, inadequate, or inappropriate. This is the symptom of a disease that paralyzes readers of the Bible, be they students or active church members. They feel they are unable to read the Bible correctly on their own. Because they are convinced they will misread the Bible, they no longer dare to open the Bible. They wait for an authority—a professor, a scholar, a preacher—to teach them the "true meaning" of the text. They are convinced they need specialized training to understand the Bible. After all, is it not a difficult book? Is it not the case that its books belong to historical, cultural, and linguistic settings far removed from people today? Thus, to all those who are not experts in these fields, reading the Bible means following the interpretation of somebody else, that is, trying to find in the text the teaching previously learned from an authority in biblical study. But since they know the teaching of a biblical text before reading it, why should they bother to read it?

Evidence of this widespread disease is everywhere. Most students in Bible study classes—in undergraduate college or in seminary—arrive without any knowledge of the Bible. They have never read it on their own. Worse, the best students often leave a class after barely skimming the biblical book under study because their primary concern is to learn "about the text" following certain scholarly interpretations of it. Similarly, in many mainline churches, most people in the pews rarely read the Bible on their own, if at all. They wait for the preachers to tell them what its teaching is. Nonspecialist would-be readers of the Bible are paralyzed.

This paralysis remains as long as one imagines: (a) that reading a biblical text has as a goal the establishment of an authoritative, comprehensive, and universally acceptable understanding of it, and (b) that the teaching that believers draw for their lives from a biblical text is legitimate only insofar as it is grounded in such an authoritative interpretation of the text. A contextual approach allows would-be readers of the Bible to overcome this paralysis by asking the participants in the study group to envision more modest goals for their reading of the Bible.

There is no reason to think that a comprehensive understanding of a biblical text—a daunting task!—is a precondition for grasping its teaching for believers today! Members of the group are right to think that they will not have this mastery of the text when they come to a roundtable. Nobody does. Biblical scholars are increasingly recognizing that a comprehensive understanding of any biblical text is impossible; as we shall see, they use many critical methods, each exclusively focused on some aspect or dimension of the text. Thus, no interpretation can claim to be comprehensive. Biblical scholars also acknowledge that no interpretation is truly objective or universal; even their most sophisticated interpretations are marked by the scholars' particular religious and cultural perspectives. In other words, all interpretations are more or less contextual. Believers should not, therefore, wait for "authoritative interpretations" before looking for the teaching of the scriptural text for their own lives.

A contextual approach starts from the recognition that, for believers, the teaching of a biblical text is never abstract. This teaching is the way in which the biblical text *as Scripture* affects their lives. Thus, for each particular believer, the teaching of a given biblical text constantly changes together with the circumstances of her or his life. For instance, although Christian believers pray the Lord's Prayer (see Matt. 6:9-13), the words can have very different meanings. If believers are in a happy situation and all the petitions seem to be on their way to fulfillment by "Our Father in heaven," the prayer tends to become a celebration God's power and glory.

If believers are in a tragic situation, "Thy kingdom come" becomes a desperate cry for help or an expression of hope that God will drastically intervene and change the dire situation.

In this scriptural reading, those who best know the situation in a given context are those who are in the best position to formulate the teaching of a text for the life of believers in it. Thus, any member of a Bible study group is in a unique position to say "what teaching of a biblical text is for believers" in a concrete situation that she or he knows well. From the start of the first roundtable discussion, any participant is in a position to contribute her or his contextual interpretation, which, together with those of the other members of the group, shows the wealth of teachings the text offers for believers in different situations. Then, in subsequent round-tables, members of the group are in a position to gain a critical perspective on their respective interpretations by comparing them with other interpretations, including scholarly ones. Group members can self-consciously assume responsibility for their choice of an interpretation, making sure it is a reading of the text that is intellectually honest and ethically accountable.

A Roadmap of the Contextual Bible Study Proposed in This Book

In the following chapters, this book invites you as a member of a Bible study group to prepare yourself for three roundtable discussions on three different passages of the Gospel of Matthew (5:3-12, 15:21-28, 28:16-20, as parts of larger sections of the Gospel) and a concluding roundtable on the Gospel of Matthew as a whole.

Why did we choose to focus this first volume of a contextual introduction to the New Testament on the Gospel of Matthew? Simply because it is the Gospel to which Christian believers throughout history and today turn most often in their quest for a biblical teaching for their lives—our concern in each roundtable.

The first roundtable on each text will be devoted to a comparison of the "teachings for contemporary believers" that the members of each group have identified. (A larger group is best divided in small groups of six to ten people.) In preparation for this discussion, each group member formulates a contextual teaching of the assigned text. For this, each member needs to envision a concrete situation for which this text offers helpful instructions for particular believers who live in this context. The more specific and realistic the envisioned situation of the believers, the easier it is to formulate the teaching of this text for these believers, that is, the way in which they are affected by this text. In addition, to facilitate the roundtable discussion, you need to prepare yourself to compare your interpretations with those of other members of the group. For this, you are invited to clarify some of the choices you made when you formulated the teaching of the text for believers in this setting.

Chapter 1 invites you to *prepare* a first roundtable on the Beatitudes (Matt. 5:3-12). The chapter will: (a) further explain why a contextual approach is helpful and the kind of questions one needs to have in mind to formulate the teaching of the Beatitudes for believers in a particular situation, and (b) help you raise a first set of questions about your interpretation, questions that will help you compare your interpretations with others. Rather than presenting abstractly how to prepare this first roundtable, this chapter guides you step-by-step as you prepare the discussion of your contextual interpretations of the Beatitudes. After the roundtable discussion, one group member is invited to prepare a concluding report to be shared with the other members and with the larger group. Chapter 1 concludes with a series of questions for preparing this report.

The second roundtable on each text invites you to *compare* your contextual interpretations with a set of existing published interpretations. In preparation, you need to compare your interpretation with these.

Chapter 2 explains the rationale for a second roundtable and provides the tools for preparing it. Once again, instead of an abstract methodological presentation, the chapter guides you through your own preparation of a second roundtable on the Beatitudes. To facilitate this comparative work, we, the authors of this book, deliberately selected existing interpretations that have quite different perspectives on the text, in part because they were developed in distinct religious and cultural contexts and were explicitly or implicitly envisioned for teaching believers with different needs. By comparing interpretations, one can readily see both the features of the text that each published interpretation views as the most significant and the theological concepts that each emphasizes. Among these, we include at least two scholarly interpretations that make use of distinct critical methods. In preparation for the discussion, by comparing your own interpretation with those presented in this chapter, you are invited to identify the features of the text you find most significant and the theological concepts you choose to emphasize. You are then ready to contribute to the second roundtable discussion. Chapter 2 concludes with a series of questions for preparing a report on the results of the discussion.

The third roundtable on each text invites you to *assess* the relative value of each of the interpretations that have been discussed, including those presented in chapter 2 and those of the group members. Once again, it is a contextual issue.

Chapter 3 explains why a third and different roundtable is needed and invites you to prepare the third roundtable on the interpretations of the Beatitudes discussed in the two preceding roundtables. In preparation for the discussion, you are asked to consider a particular situation that is described in some detail and to consider a series of questions. Another set of questions for preparing a report on the discussion concludes the chapter.

After these three roundtables on the Beatitudes, you do not need as many pointers to ensure rich and fruitful discussions. Thus, the following chapters can be more concise. Each subsequent chapter invites you to prepare three roundtables either on another passage of Matthew (15:21-28 or 28:16-20)—in chapters 4 and 5—or on the entire Gospel—in chapter 6.

The goal of approaching Bible study through a set of roundtable discussions is not to reach a conclusion about which interpretation is the best in all circumstances, but to recognize that which is best in a particular situation to particular people. This corporate process of preparation, comparison, and assessment within a context of respectful sharing can be called "scriptural criticism," that is, a disciplined effort to study the relative values of interpretations of the Bible as Scripture in an intellectually honest and ethically accountable way.

Teacher's Guide

We presuppose a pedagogy in which the teacher is primarily a leader or facilitator, playing the same role as we, the authors, are playing. As a facilitator, the teacher is a participant like any other participant in the roundtables (as described below). The teacher also provides leadership through a twofold expertise.

A) First, the teacher as leader understands the overall pedagogical process proposed in this contextual introduction to the New Testament. The leader can gain this expertise by reading the book ahead of time—since much is explained regarding it pedagogical choices in the next three chapters—or by having participated in a contextual study group led by someone else. It is also useful for the leader to have a more systematic understanding of the methodology and pedagogy upon which this contextual introduction is based.[1]

Our pedagogical process involves three kinds of roundtable discussions. The first roundtable focuses on the differences among the contextual interpretations of a Bible passage that the members of the group have prepared ahead of time for purpose of discussion. The second roundtable asks how these participants' interpretations compare with scholarly interpretations, sermons, and artistic interpretations (in literature and in visual arts). Since it has become clear by the end of the second roundtable that a choice among several interpretations must be made, participants at the third roundtable debate the question: What is the best interpretation of this Bible passage in a given life context? The leader should be fully aware of the specific goals of each of these roundtables. A reading of the entire book before the first session provides all the needed information.

B) Second, the teacher as leader will often be aware of many more interpretations of the biblical text than are the participants in the Bible study group. If the leader is a biblical scholar, she or he will know the history of scholarship and should be ready to answer questions from participants concerning the differences among scholarly interpretations.

Yet, it is essential to avoid lecturing. Any comments on scholarly interpretations should have the clear goal of facilitating the discussion by showing how these scholarly interpretations provide alternative ways of reading the text in a responsible way. If leaders are not biblical scholars, they may want to prepare themselves by consulting a review of the scholarship to help them become aware of a few *different* scholarly interpretations.[2]

According to the length of the sessions and the type of Bible study group, the leader may plan from six to twelve sessions.

If the sessions are two hours long, six sessions are sufficient: one session per chapter. There are three essential conditions: (A) Participants must come to each session well prepared (an additional introductory session might be needed for some groups on the topic of the book's introduction). (B) The larger Bible study group must be subdivided in small roundtable discussion groups to be sure that each participant has a chance to speak. A good rule of thumb is that each participant needs at least five minutes. Thus, roundtable groups of six are ideal for thirty-minute roundtable discussion periods; groups of four are ideal for twenty-minute periods. (C) A clear schedule must be set and respected to ensure there is enough time for both roundtable discussions and sharing. This schedule (and the size of roundtable discussion groups) will need to be adjusted for each chapter. Each session corresponding to chapters 1, 2, and 3 requires a single roundtable discussion time. The roundtable groups can be relatively large, as there is more time for discussion. Chapters 4, 5, and 6 require two roundtable discussion times, as well as two sharing times; since each of the roundtable discussions will be shorter, the groups will need to be smaller.

If the sessions are fifty minutes long—the usual length of university, seminary, and church adult Sunday school classes—the number of sessions needs to be doubled. The two sessions on chapters 1, 2, and 3 are best divided as: one session fully devoted to the roundtable discussion in groups (which can then include nine or ten participants); and a second session taking the form of a plenary sharing and discussion of the results of the preceding roundtable discussions. Since chapters 4, 5, and 6 require two roundtable discussions, it is best to devote each session to a roundtable discussion and the sharing of its results. In such cases, the roundtable discussion is limited to thirty minutes (six participants per roundtable group) to have twenty minutes of sharing.

In a university or seminary setting, the professor may want to add a number of lecture sessions, requiring students to read the scholars' commentaries or essays to which this book refers.[3]

Notes

1. A concise presentation of the pedagogy is found in Daniel Patte's book, *The Challenge of Discipleship: A Critical Study of the Sermon on the Mount as Scripture* (Harrisburg, Pa.: Trinity Press International, 1999), 211-34. The entire book is another example of this pedagogy. The hermeneutical, exegetical, and theological/ethical justification for this overall approach, scriptural criticism, is found in the essay by Cristina Grenholm and Daniel Patte, "Overture: Reception, Critical Interpretations, and Scriptural Criticism," in *Reading Israel in Romans: Legitimacy and Plausibility of Divergent Interpretations* (Harrisburg, Pa.: Trinity Press International, 2000), 1-54.

2. For Matthew, in addition to commentaries published since 1980, one might want to consult Graham Stanton, "The Origin and Purpose of Matthew's Gospel: Matthean Scholarship from 1945–1980." ANRW II. 25. 3. Berlin: Walter de Gruyter, 1983. More generally, see John K. Riches, A Century of New Testament Study (Harrisburg, Pa.: Trinity Press International, 1993). Other resources include: "Matthew" in *The New Interpreter's Bible*, vol. 8 (Nashville: Abingdon Press, 1995), 87-505; and *The Interpreter's Dictionary of the Bible* (Nashville: Abingdon Press, 1962).

3. The overall Bible study class should not exceed 60 participants—a lower number is better! Subdividing a large class is preferred so as to ensure that all members have the possibility of being full participants in roundtable and in plenary sessions.

CHAPTER 1

Reading the Beatitudes Ourselves: Matthew 5:3-12

In this contextual Bible study, participation in each roundtable is a three-stage process, preparation, discussion, and sharing the results. (1) Preparation: each member needs to prepare for contributing to the roundtable; (2) discussion with active contribution of each; and (3) sharing the results with other groups or the instructor. Consequently, following an introductory part, this chapter (about the first roundtable), as well as chapters 2 and 3 (about the second and the third roundtables), has three parts:

1. Preparing for the Roundtable;
2. Holding the Roundtable Discussion;
3. Sharing the Results of the Roundtable.

Introduction: Goals of a First Roundtable on a Bible Passage

This first section provides a guide and tools for preparing for a first roundtable on any Bible passage, here, on Matthew 5:3-12 (chapters 1, 2, and 3), on 15:21-28 (chapter 4), 28:16-20 (chapter 5), or on the Gospel of Matthew as a whole (chapter 6).

Why a Roundtable About the Diverse Interpretations of the Members of the Group?

People who study the Bible already know intuitively, or from experience, that:

- Believers of different traditions *disagree about the meaning* of any biblical passage. They have *divergent scriptural interpretations;*
- Most of these disagreements arise because scriptural interpretations are particular to *believers in specific life contexts;* and
- Quite a few of these interpretations are *problematic and even dangerous.*

These are good reasons to discuss different readings of the Gospel of Matthew and to begin with the Beatitudes.

Everyone wants to avoid or challenge what he or she perceives as problematic and dangerous interpretations. Who would not? Intuitively, each of us senses that such interpretations are often misleading and confusing. They clash with our convictions. They must be wrong. Even more disturbing is the fact that such interpretations of the Bible have been used to condone or instigate violence, cruelty, and oppression. Interpretations of the Bible have led to religious wars; Crusades, with the massacres of Jewish and Muslim "infidels"; persecution and killing of heretics; slavery; and anti-Semitism and the Jewish Holocaust. Interpretations of the Bible have encouraged submission to oppressive political systems—apartheid in South Africa, racism, and the oppression and marginalization of women. Interpretations of the Bible have supported active participation in oppressive economic systems. They marginalize people from different cultures. And, unfortunately, the list of bad effects of biblical interpretations is much longer.

Intuitively, most of us feel that such interpretations are bad or wrong. But obviously, for some (many!) people they are not wrong; rather, they are welcomed as the proper understanding of God's Word, indeed, as the very Word of God. It was in the name of God that Christians holding such interpretations of Scripture massacred Jewish and Muslim "infidels."

The fact is that any interpretation of Scripture has, for better or for worse, an amazing power and authority for believers. It can bring peace and wholeness, but it can also tear apart and destroy both individual believers and their congregations and denominations. Interpretations of the Bible can drive believers and their congregations to the services of others and can also drive them to perpetrate the most atrocious physical and psychological abuses.

One solution, of course, would be—and has often been—to dismiss all scriptural readings and, ultimately, to stop reading the Bible as Scripture. To use a cliché, this would be throwing the baby out with the bath water! The destructive abuses of Scripture should not overshadow its constructive uses. What is needed is "scriptural criticism," that is, a way to assess the relative values of different scriptural interpretations, and in this way discern which interpretations are "bad" and which are "good."

For believers, this is clear. It does not make any sense to deprive oneself of the Word of God as an essential resource in the struggle with evil. Scripture remains an essential resource for the Christian, even (or especially) when evil takes the form of a (mis)use of Scripture. Jesus did not abandon Scripture— the Word that offers essential nourishment—even after Satan misused Scripture in the temptation (Matt. 4:1-11). Instead, Jesus corrected the devil's misuse of Scripture by quoting another biblical text. In sum, it is myopic to dismiss Scripture because of the destructive abuses of it.

It is also myopic to dismiss or ignore the scriptural readings by believers—including sermons and devotional readings by ordinary believers— or to consider all such readings as suspect until proved true. What are substituted by default are the interpretations of the experts, usually biblical scholars trained in U.S. and European academic institutions. Their interpretations are then viewed as the benchmark over against which the believers' scriptural readings should be assessed. For sure, many dangerously warped interpretations are screened in this way. And this is fine. Many other possibly more helpful interpretations are also excluded, merely because they reflect cultural contexts other than those of the European American university.

The systematic exclusion and silencing of interpretations developed in other cultures, as well as those interpretations of so-called minority subcultures and nonscholarly readers, contributes to the very problem we strive to overcome. There is something very wrong when a biblical interpretation is excluded as illegitimate simply because it is African or Filipino or African American or feminist (from a woman's perspective) or nonscholarly! Such elitist and exclusivist attitudes are not tolerated in many secular societies today. For readers of the Bible, we can put it most bluntly by quoting the exclamation and question that Paul addressed to the arrogant Corinthians. Its biting rebuke directly applies to Western scholars—primarily males—who present their interpretations as a norm: "What! Did the word of God originate with you, or are you the only ones it has reached?" (1 Cor. 14:36 RSV).

This is not to say that scholarly interpretations should be ignored. As we shall see, they have an essential role in helping us gain a critical perspective on other biblical interpretations. But, at the beginning of our study, we must acknowledge the existence of numerous scriptural interpretations. We must also have a positive, rather than negative, attitude toward all of them. Instead of looking with suspicion at interpretations that are different from ours, we should assume that any interpretation is *legitimate* until proved otherwise.

The fact that there are many different scriptural interpretations of the same passage is not a sign that most of these interpretations are wrong. Scriptural interpretations by definition express the teaching of the text *as it applies to the lives of believers in a particular life context*. It is to be expected that such scriptural interpretations of a biblical passage for believers *in different life contexts* will be as different as these life contexts. Furthermore, scriptural interpretations of a biblical passage by believers who have different *religious or secular experiences* will be as different as their experiences and theological concerns. The number of scriptural interpretations is a testimony to the richness of the Bible. Somehow, the same passage addresses the wide spectrum of needs of both believers and their neighbors, both near and far.

Given this diversity in scriptural interpretations, in preparation for the first roundtable, we ask you to formulate your own scriptural interpretation and to keep in mind that it is a contextual interpretation. Any member of a Bible study group is in a position to identify a life context in which believers might benefit from the teaching of the assigned biblical passage—for example, Matthew 5:3-12. Any member can then prepare herself or himself to contribute to the roundtable discussion by formulating the teaching of the assigned passage for those Christians in whatever particular life context they have identified as addressed by the biblical passage—whether or not the group participants are themselves believers.

Preparing Your Contribution to a First Roundtable

All participants in the group, including participants who are not Christian believers, are now ready to prepare a contextual scriptural interpretation of any assigned Bible passage. Everyone can identify a life context in which the Beatitudes might be important for Christians, and everyone can also formulate the teaching for that life context. It is not a matter of spelling out the overall "meaning of the text"—conceived either as "what the text says" to everyone who reads it, or as "what the text meant" for its original readers. A contextual, scriptural interpretation is simply concerned in formulating *the teaching of this text for believers in a particular life context*—in short, its *"teaching for* believers" or simply its "teaching."

Every participant in the first roundtable is expected to make a contribution to the discussion by formulating the teaching of the text for certain believers. No one should be reluctant to make such a contribution for fear of being wrong. If the discussions are "roundtable" discussions, such a fear is without foundation for two reasons.

First, in such roundtable discussion, *all* interpretations of the Bible are *legitimate* interpretations until proved otherwise. You should not hesitate to share your thoughts about the teaching for Christian believers of an assigned Bible passage, such as the Beatitudes (Matt. 5:3-12). It is not difficult to provide an interpretation that is welcomed by the group and stands the test of discussion. You should simply make clear that your interpretation is *scriptural* by underscoring how the teaching of this Bible passage addresses the needs of believers in a particular life context. This is an exercise in *contextual interpretation*, as explained below.

Second, these are "roundtable discussions." The shape of the table is important! Every participant is equal to every other participant at this "round" table. The later section "A First Roundtable Discussion" provides some simple ground rules.

An Exercise in Contextual Interpretation

Preparing your contribution to a first roundtable is an exercise in contextual interpretation each time. This exercise follows the pattern found in many ancient and modern manuals for interpreting the Bible as Scripture. You should prepare a written contribution for the roundtable discussion on the assigned passage of Matthew. You should:

- read the assigned passage for the first time in a translation of your native language (for example, for an English translation readers might choose the New Revised Standard Version or New International Version; in the Philippines, a participant might want to use a translation in Cebuano, Ilokano, or Tagalog);
- envision a present-day life context for Christians in which this text could provide guidance (this involves making a choice because, in most instances, several such situations can be envisioned);
- identify the needs (individual or collective, religious or physical) that Christians or their neighbors in this situation have; and
- reread the assigned text with the goal of finding how this Scripture passage addresses these needs (or, negatively, how this Bible passage ignores these needs or even exacerbates them).

Identifying a present-day situation in which Christians or their neighbors have needs that can truly be addressed by the assigned text demands that you consider several situations and clarify the needs or problems faced by believers in these situations. By identifying a present-day situation, readers can discern what life contexts are addressed by the assigned Bible passage and, if several possibilities emerge, which of these situations and teachings are most important.

In order to clarify the needs or problems faced by believers, you should consider a contemporary situation, simply to ensure that the interpretation is relevant to real flesh and blood believers. The interpretation of this Bible passage should *matter* for someone, somewhere, today. Once a contemporary situation has been identified, to which the biblical passage may speak, then the needs or problems of that situation can be clarified by asking the following questions:

1) **What aspects of the believers' lives do these needs concern?** Is it private or individual life? Is it family life? Is it church life? Is it social life (at work, at school, at play)? Is it cultural life (with its vision of the purpose of life, its values, its ideologies, philosophies)? Is it life in relationship with people of different religions or faiths or without any at all? Then, when you have described the concrete needs and problems that believers face in this situation, you should be ready to ask more specific questions regarding the nature of the believers' needs so as to clarify what problem the Bible passage might address.

2) **What is the root problem in this life context?** Is the problem a lack of knowledge? If so, a lack of what kind of knowledge? Is the problem a lack of ability? If so, a lack of ability to do what? Is the problem a lack of will? If so, a lack of will to do what? Is the problem a lack of vision or faith? If so, a lack of what kind of vision?

These questions prompt you to reread the Bible text with a very clear focus. If, for instance, the believers' need is at root a "lack of knowledge of God's will regarding what they should do in a particular situation," then the question is whether or not the text says anything regarding God's will. Similarly, if the root problem is a sense of powerlessness (a lack of ability), then you should identify how this passage could empower believers or their neighbors. But perhaps Christians in this life situation both know God's will and are able to do it. Is the problem, then, perhaps that, for one reason or another, they do not want to do God's will? In such a case, you should read the text to find out how it might entice or convince believers to do God's will. Finally, the believers' problem might be doubt, lack of faith, not believing (in God), or not seeing the presence of God. Then the question is: Does this text communicate faith to doubting believers? If so, how? For instance, how does it share with them a vision of the coming kingdom and its presence? Keeping in mind that faith or vision is often communicated by rituals, the question may be: In what ritual (for example, prayer, acts such as "blessing" or "cursing," or dramatic story-telling, as well as liturgical acts and worship services) does the Bible passage invite readers to share its vision or faith?

These are only a few general suggestions. They will become more specific with each assigned passage. Yet, they should be enough to make clear that any member of any Bible study group, whether or not she or he is a Christian, can formulate such a contextual scriptural teaching of the passage. **Preparation for a first roundtable is simply a matter of *envisioning* how this text *would address* the needs that Christians might have in particular circumstances.**

A First Roundtable Discussion

Because each participant has prepared a written summary of the teaching of the assigned passage of Matthew for believers in a specific contemporary life context, the first roundtable on each biblical passage will be more clearly focused. It is also useful for you to have your written interpretations available for distribution to all members of the group so that you will not be tempted to modify or abandon your interpretations during the discussion—for instance, because the interpretation presented by someone else seems better. The contribution of the individual interpretations is their differences! You should not abandon your interpretations. To do so would withdraw your contributions from the group discussion. The following ground rules should make the roundtable much less threatening, even for the most apprehensive participants:

- In a *round*table discussion, the shape of the table is important. Everyone sitting around this table has equal rights and authority. There is no position at the head of the table. The interpretation of any given member of the group is as important and valuable as that of any other member of the group.
- Everyone sitting around this table is expected to make a contribution to the discussion by bringing to it her or his interpretation of an assigned Bible passage, emphasizing its teaching for particular Christians in a present-day context. Your interpretation makes a genuine contribution to the discussion when you bring to the conversation something *different,* as compared with the interpretations of other members of the group. This readily happens when each interpretation explicitly envisions the concrete life situation of the believers who would benefit from the teaching of this scriptural text.
- The goal of the roundtable is to bring to light the broad range of

"teachings for believers" that the assigned passage offers for those who read this text as Scripture.

Each participant will have something different to contribute to the roundtable. The goal is to acknowledge the particular insights that each interpretation brings to the group's appreciation for the richness of the assigned passage. You should remember that a desire for respect of one's own opinion requires respect for the opinions of others.

The roundtable should demonstrate that *differences* among interpretations produce valuable insights. You cannot claim to respect someone else's interpretation if you cannot say how the other interpretation differs from your own and vice versa. By adopting this attitude in roundtable discussions, members of the group begin to gain a critical distance from their own interpretations and those of others. They abandon the uncritical (and, in most instances, unethical), offhanded dismissal of all readings that do not conform to their own.

Such a focus also prevents participants from making the uncritical claim that their own readings are the only possible ones because "this is what the text says" or "faithful interpreters have no choice." At minimum, you should realize that the Bible passage will address different believers with different needs in different contexts, differently. The "teaching for believers" of a text read as Scripture is always contextual. Thus, it is useful to focus part of the roundtable on the life situations envisioned in each interpretation and on the different needs and problems that believers face in these contexts. It is important to recognize explicitly that each member of the group has made *contextual choices* in formulating the teaching of the text for these believers. Regarding your interpretation, you should be ready to say:

- What aspect(s) of the believers' particular life context is most helpfully addressed by this Bible passage (private life, family life, church life, social life, cultural and political life, relations of people with different religious convictions); and
- What is the root problem that believers face in this context and that the Bible passage helps them address (lack of knowledge, of ability, of will, of faith or vision).

Making Explicit the Views of Scripture
Presupposed by Each Interpretation

In preparation for the first roundtable, it is also helpful to take note of an implicitly broad *theological choice* in each interpretation. (Theological choices will be one of the primary concerns of the second roundtables; see chapter 2). Even without realizing it, you have emphasized one view of the role of Scripture in the lives of believers over another. Each interpretation seeking to discern the teaching of a Bible passage for believers presupposes that the Bible affects these believers in certain ways. A listing of some important options will facilitate preparation for this part of the roundtable discussion, even if the views of Scripture held by some members of the group are not found on this partial list. Each view of Scripture is represented by a more or less traditional metaphor.

- Scripture as a **Lamp to My Feet** and Light for My Path (Psalm 119:105); a Compass for Life; a Law; a Guide for Life

According to this view, Scripture teaches believers what they should do, step by step, because they lack direction for their lives and do not know what is good or evil. Here, the biblical text provides **knowledge** of what believers are called by God to do.

- Scripture as **Canon**; a measure for assessing behavior or life; a law for the community of believers

According to this view, Scripture shapes the believers' moral life as an implementation of God's will, so that the church may fulfill its mission. Scripture provides a means to recognize who does or does not belong to the community of believers. The Bible either provides **knowledge** of what believers must do to belong to the community or, through threats and demands, influences a believer's **will** to act in a certain way and to contribute to the mission of the church.

- Scripture as **Good News**; loving word of a parent

According to this view, Scripture is a revelation of God's love. It is a comforting, encouraging, merciful word that helps believers experience God's love, grace, and mercy. The Bible provides believers **knowledge** of God's love, or influences their **will** to serve God, as a response to God's love.

- Scripture as **Book of the Covenant** (or testament); **Family Album**

According to this view, Scripture establishes and reinforces one's identity and vocation as a member of God's people (as the family of God). It provides a true sense of the believer's relationship to others and to God. The

Bible first establishes a believer's **faith** or **vision** of his or her identity as a member of God's people or family. Second, it establishes a believer's **will** to act accordingly.

- Scripture as **Corrective Glasses**; promise or prophecy; incarnated Word

According to this view, Scripture allows believers to see their lives or experiences through eyes of faith, discerning in the midst of evil "what is good and acceptable and perfect" and what God is doing as fulfillment of promises or prophecies. The Bible provides **faith or a vision** of God's presence in the lives of believers and **empowers or enables** them, or influences their **will,** to imitate God.

- Scripture as **Empowering Word**

According to this view, Scripture conjures a new reality for believers. For example, it brings about preliminary manifestations of the kingdom and of God's justice in a broken world. It provides hope for the present situation of otherwise powerless believers. It **empowers and enables** believers to struggle for the kingdom and God's justice.

- Scripture as **Holy Bible**

According to this view, Scripture confronts believers with the holy. The Bible provides a "goose bumps" experience—a sense of awe, mystery, and wonder—because it shatters the believers' expectations and confronts them with something radically different and awe inspiring. The Bible provides renewed **faith or vision** for the believer's life in the presence of God.

This list hardly exhausts the possible metaphors for the relationships between Scripture and the lives of believers. You should feel free to formulate other metaphors for the particular role of Scripture as you recognize them in interpretations around the table and in your own interpretations.

The following form will assist you in preparing yourself for any first roundtable discussion of any Bible passage. *Note: Make several copies of this blank form for later use.* Refer to chapter 1 for more detailed instructions regarding each question.

Form for Roundtable 1: Preparing a Contextual Interpretation

Part A: Identify a context in which (the assigned Bible passage) _____ **is relevant to the lives of Christians today.**

1. Briefly describe this situation as *concretely* as possible:

2. What verses or phrases are relevant to this particular situation? (Quote the most important verses or phrases.)

3. Identify the needs of Christians in this context.

a) Where in the believers' lives do these needs most often occur, or what part of life do they most directly affect? Choose the primary need (make a choice): (a) private life? (b) family life? (c) church life? (d) social life (at work, at school, in their leisure time)? (e) cultural and political life (with its vision of the purpose of life, its values, its ideologies, its philosophies)? (f) life in relationship with people of other religions and faiths? (g) another area of life (explain)?
YOUR ANSWER (with explanation):

b) What is the primary root problem that these Christians encounter in this context and that the Bible passage should address? (Remember that a problem may concern Christians directly or may concern their neighbors. If the latter, then the question may be how the Christians should relate to their neighbors.) Choose the primary root problem (make a choice): (a) A lack of **knowledge**? What kind? Who lacks this knowledge? (b) A lack of **ability**? To do what? Who lacks this ability? (c) A lack of **will**? To do what? Who lacks this will? (d) A lack of **faith** or **vision**? What kind? Who lacks this vision or faith?
YOUR ANSWER (with explanation):

Part B: The Teaching of (the assigned Bible passage) _____ for believers in the context described in Part A

1. Summarize the teaching of this passage for Christians in this context. Reread the Bible passage, keeping in mind the needs, especially the root problem, described in Part A. Formulate the teaching of this Bible passage by completing the following sentence (mentioning verses and phrases of the text that contain this teaching):

"The main teaching of this Scripture for these believers' lives as Christians in this context is _____ ."

2. The Role of Scripture. What is the role of Scripture presupposed above by the formulation of the teaching of the text for these particular believers in this particular context? What would be the most appropriate metaphor for this role of the text of Scripture? Explain how this teaching of the text for believers performs this role.

See the list of metaphors in chapter 1 for specific options.

YOUR ANSWER (with explanation):

Part C: Personal assessment

Since the Christian envisioned above may be very different from any of the participants in the Bible study group, two additional questions are appropriate and necessary:

1. What did you personally learn from this text? What was new and surprising (positively or negatively) in this text for you?
YOUR ANSWER (with brief explanation):

2. How do you personally rate the value of this teaching for the needs of the Christians described above. Is it a "good" (i.e., helpful, effective) teaching for overcoming the problem in their lives? Can you envision a "better" teaching (for instance, on the basis of different Bible passages or different religions and philosophies)? Does the assigned Bible passage lead to a dubious understanding of the "real" problem in this situation? Does it propose a solution to the problem that is dangerous and could be devastating for the people involved?
YOUR ANSWER (with explanation):

I—Preparing for a First Roundtable on the Beatitudes (Matt. 5:3-12)[1]

Many Christians read the Beatitudes as Scripture and find in them a "teaching for their lives" in very different contexts. Yet this teaching of the Beatitudes varies from believer to believer.

This plurality of teachings arises in part because Christians read the Beatitudes as Scripture, that is, as a living Word that addresses them in the concrete realities of their lives. Believers who read a text as Scripture bring the text to bear on their lives and, conversely, bring their needs, problems, and concerns to bear on the text. The diversity of teachings found in the Beatitudes shows the richness of a text that can address the needs of Christians in vastly different life contexts. Thus, one of the first tasks of this Bible study group is to discover the richness of the Beatitudes by identifying this range of teachings.

For this purpose, the group needs the contributions of all of its members—including those of the leader or facilitator. Everyone brings to the table a distinctive interpretation of the teaching of the Beatitudes. In preparation, you are invited to reread the Beatitudes in order to identify a present-day situation in the experience of Christians *for which this text is relevant.* (This involves *making a choice,* since the text is relevant to several such life contexts). For this contextual reading, we first ask you to clarify the needs or problems that Christians face in this context. Then, after reading the Beatitudes again, we ask you to formulate the teaching that this text has for these believers in the particular situation you have chosen.

Matthew 5:3-12 (NRSV and alternate translations)

Some differences in interpretation reflect the fact that Christian believers use different translations of the Greek text in their own native languages. The following quotation from the Beatitudes suggests some of these alternative English translations proposed by interpreters discussed in chapter 2.

5:3 "Blessed [Happy, Helped] are the poor in spirit, for theirs is the kingdom of heaven [for them God reigns]."

5:4 "Blessed [Happy, Helped] are those who mourn, for they will be comforted."

5:5 "Blessed [Happy, Helped] are the meek, for they will inherit the earth [land]."

5:6 "Blessed [Happy, Helped] are those who hunger and thirst for righteousness [justice], for they will be filled [eat their fill]."

5:7 "Blessed [Happy, Helped] are the merciful [compassionate], for they will receive mercy [compassion]."

5:8 "Blessed [Happy, Helped] are the pure [open, clear of shame] in heart, for they will see God."

5:9 "Blessed [Happy, Helped] are the peacemakers, for they will be called children of God."

5:10 "Blessed [Happy, Helped] are those who are persecuted for righteousness' [justice's] sake, for theirs is the kingdom of heaven [for them God reigns]."

5:11 "Blessed [Happy, Helped] are you when people revile you and persecute you and utter all kinds of evil against you falsely on my account."

5:12 "Rejoice and be glad, for your reward is [your wages are] great in heaven, for in the same way they persecuted the prophets who were before you."

A) Identifying a Contemporary Context in Which Matthew 5:3-12 Is Relevant to the Lives of Christians

To facilitate the discussion, we propose that everyone focus on the teaching of the Beatitudes **for Christians and their lives as disciples.** Choose a specific situation for which the passage seems to speak.

1. Can we envision a specific life context in which this Bible passage might have a teaching for Christians about their lives as disciples? At first, we might wonder. But as soon as we begin to picture in our minds believers who, in concrete situations, have some kind of need or problem, we discover that the Beatitudes inform many different situations in life. This problem or need may be one that is directly of concern to the Christians or related to the world in which the believers live. For this exercise in contextual interpretation, you should make a choice: What is the specific situation in life for which this passage would be the most helpful to Christians? Briefly describe this life context as concretely as possible. (For this, you may wish to use "Form for Roundtable 1.") This exercise will prepare you to make an important contribution to the study group.

2. It will be helpful for the roundtable discussion also to specify what verses or phrases in Matthew 5:3-12 suggest that the text is relevant to this particular life situation.

3. Before formulating the teaching of the Beatitudes for believers in this context, we need a clear idea of the needs they have. This kind of reflection is also a good preparation for the roundtable discussion. We find the following questions to be most helpful in clarifying these needs:

(a) What is the *primary* aspect of the believer's life where these needs or problems arise? (We must make a choice.)

> (1) private life? (2) family life? (3) church life? (4) social life (at work, at school, in leisure time)? (5) cultural and political life (with its vision of the purpose of life, its values, its ideologies, its philosophies)? (6) life in relationship with people of different religions and faiths? (7) another area of life? (Be specific.)

(b) What is the *primary root problem* that these Christians face in this situation and that the Bible passage should address? (Whether it concerns the Christians directly or concerns other people around them; if the latter, then, for these believers, the question may be how they can meet the needs of others in this situation.) Again, make a choice; be specific.

> (1) A lack of **knowledge**? (What kind? Who lacks this knowledge?) (2) A lack of **ability**? (To do what? Who lacks this ability?) (3) A lack of **will**? (To do what? Who lacks this will?) (4) A lack of **faith or vision**? (What kind? Who lacks this vision or faith?)

B) What Is the Teaching of Matthew 5:3-12 for Christians and Their Lives as Disciples in This Context?

1. Now we are ready to formulate the teaching of this text for Christians and their lives as disciples in this situation. It may help to reread Matthew 5:3-12, keeping in mind the needs already specified above. The question now is: How do the Beatitudes actually address these needs? Again, we focus on the main teaching that this text has for the situation. This means, once again, that each of us must make a choice. Preparing ourselves for a roundtable discussion, in which everyone is supposed to speak, requires each of us to choose a specific teaching that, for one reason or another, seems to be the most important one. Every member of the group will have the opportunity to present his or her choice for the main teaching of the Beatitudes.

As we formulate the significance of this text for Christians in this particular life context, we should remember that the *teaching* of a scriptural text for believers is necessarily *new* for them, even if they already know "what the text says." Repeating "what the text says" is not yet expressing "the teaching of this text" *for believers in a particular life context*. These believers have not learned anything if they do not receive from this text: either *new* insights into their life context—a renewal of the mind allowing them to discern both what is problematic and "what is good, acceptable, and perfect" in their situation (cf. Rom. 12:2)—or *new* insights into the text—including in the present case what it says about a life of discipleship—as the text is reread from the perspective of this particular life context. This teaching is new for these believers in the sense that it addresses a problem they really have in a particular life context and that, without the help of the text, they could not address in the same way.

It will be helpful for the roundtable discussion also to specify what verses or phrases in Matthew 5:3-12 address this problem or need most directly and in a new way.

2. In preparation for the first roundtable discussion, we should also take note of what role we assume for Scripture (an issue we will discuss further at the second roundtable). Using the set of metaphors presented previously (see pp. 27-28), each of us can ponder how Scripture functions in our formulation of the teaching of the Beatitudes for certain believers. Notice how our use of Scripture depends on the need we identified as most significant in the life context of these believers.

C) Personal Assessment of This Teaching

Finally, before we engage in the first roundtable discussion, it is helpful to clarify our own stance vis-à-vis this biblical teaching. (This will be discussed further in the third roundtable). For many of us, it is quite simple: As Christians ourselves, we have identified those to whom the teaching is addressed. In fact, we may have chosen a situation closely related to our own. In such a case, we usually formulate a teaching that we regard as "good"—indeed, as the Word of God for us. But if the Christians we envisioned above are very different from ourselves, or the life context we chose is very different from ours, the task of evaluating the message of the biblical passage must proceed in a different way. This may be the case for those of us who belong to another religious tradition or who consider ourselves nonreligious. Whatever our situation, it is important to ask ourselves: How do I personally rate the value of this teaching for the needs involved in this context? Is it a "good" (i.e., helpful, effective) teaching for overcoming the problem I have identified? Can I envision a "better" teaching (for instance, on the basis of a different biblical text, or of a different religious tradition or philosophy)? In your view, does the proposed teaching lead to confusion about the real issues involved in this situation? Does it offer a solution to the problem that is dangerous and potentially devastating for the people who follow the biblical teaching or those to whom they relate?[2]

II—Holding a First Roundtable on the Beatitudes

When you have completed your answers to the questions in the section above (and have completed the form on pages 29-32), you will be prepared for your first roundtable.[3] You will have a good discussion if everyone has prepared herself or himself as you did. You will soon discover that the members of your group have perceived different teachings of the Beatitudes for believers today. This plurality exists in part because Christians read the Beatitudes as Scripture, as a Living Word that addresses them in the concrete realities of their lives. Each interpretation reflects *contextual choices* that are made on the basis of this text and that include (1) identifying a particular kind of problem or need, (2) identifying a root problem, and (3) formulating a teaching that addresses this need.

Suggestions for a Profitable Discussion

Members of the Bible study group should take turns assuming two leadership positions: facilitator and scribe.

The *facilitator* provides leadership by "facilitating" the discussion, first by making sure that everyone around the table has a chance to express herself or himself. One way to hear from the outset the voice of each one is to proceed to a collective reading of the text, each one reading a verse. Second, the facilitator should make sure that each interpretation is welcomed as an actual contribution to the discussion. It may be necessary for the facilitator to remind the group that differences among contextual interpretations are not signs that one of the interpretations is right and the other wrong, but rather signs of the richness of a scriptural text that can address the needs of Christians in vastly different life contexts. Actually, the main task of the facilitator is to make sure that the *differences* among the interpretations of the members of the group are duly noted. The facilitator may want to remind participants that it is inappropriate to say: "My interpretation of the teaching of the Beatitudes is the same as the one presented by X (another member of the group)."

More constructively, to make explicit the different perspectives present around the table, the facilitator may begin the discussion by asking each participant to briefly describe the specific concrete situation she or he has chosen. Then, in a second round, you should be given the time to present the main points of your contextual interpretations, at least Part A, about the contextual need, and Part B, about the teaching of the text that addresses this problem. Part C may become the topic of a third round of discussion. Yet, according to the group dynamics, the facilitator may choose to proceed with a single round of discussion, each participant presenting at once the three parts of her or his interpretation.

Throughout the roundtable discussion, following each participant's presentation of his or her interpretation, the facilitator should invite the other members of the group to raise any questions of clarification they may have. Two kinds of questions are pertinent; those asking for a clarification of:

1. *The consistency of the interpretation.* For instance: Is the "teaching of the Beatitudes for believers" (Part B, 1) truly addressing the need and root problem of the believers in their life context (as described in Part A)? Is the choice of need and root problem (in Part A, 3) consistent with the description of the concrete situation (in Part A, 1)? Is the choice of a role of Scripture (in Part B, 2) consistent with the formulation of teaching (in Part B, 1) and with the choice of root problem (in Part A, 3)? How do the chosen verses and phrases of the Bible passage (mentioned in Part A, 2 and Part B, 1) support the teaching (as formulated in Part B, 1)?
2. *The differences* between this interpretation and interpretations by other members of the group.

Through these questions, the members of the group following the leadership of the facilitator both affirm the value of one another's contextual interpretations in their differences and keep one another accountable for her or his interpretation.

This emphasis on "differences" may be surprising for some members of the Bible study group. It does not intend to negate similarities among interpretations, which will necessarily be numerous, since everyone deals with the same Bible passage. These similarities are so obvious for participants that they do not need to be emphasized. Furthermore, if they are the focus of the discussion, the differences would be ignored. Then, the specific contributions of each of the members of the group would also be ignored, and the richness of the text would be hidden.

The *scribe*'s responsibility is to keep the minutes of the roundtable discussion in preparation for sharing the results of the roundtable with other groups or, if there is a single group, in preparation for providing the members with a written summary of these results.

III—Sharing Results of a First Roundtable on the Beatitudes

Before proceeding with the preparation of a second roundtable on the Beatitudes, it is essential to take stock of the results of the first one. This will be done through the report prepared by the scribe of each group, both for the other members of the group (who can refer to this report in the subsequent roundtables) and for other groups (in plenary session of a large class that has been subdivided into several groups).

The goal of this report is to make clear the *differences* among the interpretations. In preparation of this report, the scribe often needs to be a very active participant in the discussion, constantly asking other members of the group to explain in which way their contextual interpretations differ. As a summary of the discussion, the scribe's report is most helpful when it underscores the differences concerning:

1) The aspect of the believers' lives, where the need found is in the chosen context (private life? family life? etc.)
2) Root problems (lack of knowledge? lack of ability? lack of will? lack of faith or vision?)
3) The ways the Bible passage addresses this need and this root problem
4) The roles of Scripture.

Additional Preparation Exercise: Comparing Your Interpretation with Augustine's Interpretation of the Beatitudes

In preparation for your role in the discussion, the class leader, the facilitator, and the scribe of the roundtable discussion (and the other members of group who are interested) may want to compare the choices they made regarding the Beatitudes with those of Augustine. In this way they will be able to anticipate the issues that need to be raised during the first roundtable.

Augustine's interpretation is a scriptural interpretation seeking to discern the teaching of the Beatitudes for Christians in his life context. It is therefore a contextual interpretation such as yours. More specific, it presents the formulation of the "teaching for believers" (as in Part B, 1 of the form you have prepared) and presupposes a life context in which believers have particular needs grounded in a root problem that the Beatitudes help them address. As you read his interpretation, you can readily identify what is *different* in Augustine's contextual choices as compared with the choices you made in your own interpretation. (To help, we have added emphases in Augustine's interpretation.)

- Regarding the aspect of life in which believers have a need, did Augustine choose a different aspect of life as compared with your choice? What is the primary location of this need for you? For Augustine? Is it private life? Family life? Church life? Social life? Cultural and political life? Life in relationship with people of other religions and faiths? (Consider especially *the words and phrases in italics* in Augustine's interpretation below, but do not limit yourself to these.)

- Did Augustine envision a different root problem as compared with the root problem, according to your interpretation, the text addresses for Christians? Is it a lack of knowledge? A lack of ability? A lack of will? A lack of faith or vision? What more specific problem? (Consider especially **the words and phrases in bold** in Augustine's interpretation below, but do not limit yourself to these.)

- How different are the teachings of the Beatitudes for believers according to Augustine and according to you? (To identify what is the teaching for believers according to Augustine, consider especially the underlined words and phrases in Augustine's interpretation below, but do not limit yourself to these.)

- In what way is the role Scripture plays for Augustine different from the role it plays for you? Which metaphor would you use to describe Augustine's view, so that the difference with your own view may be clear?

Obviously, despite the pointers we provided, each of us will emphasize particular aspects of Augustine's interpretation because they most directly express the differences between his interpretation and ours. The characteristics of Augustine's interpretation (what is for him the teaching of this text, the need and root problem it addresses, the role of Scripture) are necessarily those that are highlighted through comparison with our own interpretation. For each of us, the most significant aspects of the interpretation of someone else (of Augustine or of another member of our group) are those that are *different* from (and, secondarily, similar to) our own interpretation. This is true for all the interpretations we consider after formulating our own.

Why did we choose Augustine's interpretation for this comparison? Simply because we are quite confident that the believers' life context you envisioned is quite different from the one Augustine envisioned. Your life context is very different from his.

Saint Augustine (354–430) was a Christian theologian and Bishop of Hippo, in North Africa. He was priest and then bishop at a time when the Roman Empire was crumbling down, and morality was very low in public life. After education in philosophy, strongly influenced by the Neoplatonic philosopher Plotinus, he converted (in 387) while remaining influenced by Platonic views. For Augustine, the eternal truths as they are in God somehow supply light to the human mind, enabling it to see the necessity of moral standards. Similarly, he distinguishes the "literal" meaning of Scripture from its "spiritual" meaning, a hidden, supernatural truth.

Here is the concluding part (on Matt. 5:10) from Augustine's commentary on the Beatitudes.[4]

> The very number of the statements [beatitudes] ought to be carefully considered. For blessedness begins from humility: "Blessed are the poor in spirit" [Matt. 5:3], that is, those who are not **puffed up**, whose *soul* submits itself to divine authority for fear that it may pass on from this life to punishment, even if it should perhaps in this life seem to itself to be blessed. After that *the soul* comes to the knowledge of the divine Scriptures, where it is necessary to prove itself meek in piety so it may not dare to **disparage what seems absurd** to the unlearned, and by **stubborn controversy render itself unteachable**. From there it begins to know in what **worldly bonds** it is being **held by carnal habit and sins**. And so in this third stage, in which there is knowledge, the loss of the highest good is mourned because the *soul* is **tangled in the lowest things**. In the fourth stage, moreover, there is labor: a great effort made for the *mind* to tear itself away from those **things to which it is bound by harmful delight**. Here, therefore, justice will be hungered and thirsted for and much delight will not be let go without sadness. In the fifth stage, advice on how to get beyond that labor is given to those who have persevered in it. For unless *a person* is helped by one who is stronger, there is no way that *one alone* can extricate oneself from **such a great entanglement of miseries**. It is, moreover, a just counsel that one who wishes help from someone stronger should aid anyone who is weaker in that in which one is stronger. And so, "Blessed are the merciful, for mercy will be shown them" [Matt. 5:7]. In the sixth stage, there is purity of heart, since the *soul* is now (as a result of the <u>right conscience of good deeds</u>) in condition to contemplate that highest good which can be discerned only by the *pure and tranquil intellect*. The seventh and last stage is wisdom itself, that is, the contemplation of truth, which makes the *whole person* peaceful and which causes one to take <u>on the likeness of God</u>. It is summed up thus: "Blessed are the peacemakers, for they will be called children of God" [Matt. 5:9].
>
> The eighth maxim returns, as it were, to the beginning, for it shows forth and commends <u>what is complete and perfect</u>. And so in the first and the eighth statements the kingdom of heaven is mentioned: "Blessed are the poor in spirit, for theirs is the kingdom of heaven" [Matt. 5:3], and "Blessed are those who suffer persecution for justice's sake, for theirs is the kingdom of heaven" [Matt. 5:10]. For indeed it is said, "Who will separate us from the love of Christ: will tribulation or distress, or persecution or famine, or nakedness, or peril, or the sword?" [Rom. 8:35]. Seven in number, then, are the things which <u>bring perfection;</u> and the eighth illuminates and <u>points out what is perfect,</u> so that through these steps others might also *be* <u>made perfect,</u> starting once more, so to speak, from the beginning.

Notes

1. The preceding form allows easy comparison of your interpretation with those of other members of the group. Print the form or copy it into your word processor and complete it as you read the following paragraphs. The paragraph numbers below correspond to those on the form. The same form is to be used in preparation of the first roundtable on each assigned Bible passage.

2. The following Abingdon Press titles about Matthew are recommended to supplement this book: *The New Interpreter's Bible*, vol. 8, Matthew (available from Cokesbury at http://www.cokesbury.com/Book/product.asp?product%5 Fid=27821X&series=&type=&agelevel); *The Gospel of Matthew*, Interpreting Biblical Texts Series ((http://www.cokesbury.com/Book/product.asp?product %5Fid=008484&series=&type=&agelevel=); *Abingdon New Testament Commentary*, Matthew (http://www.cokesbury.com/Book/product.asp?product%5Fid=057663& series=&type=&agelevel=).

In addition, students may want to consult Graham Stanton, "The Origin and Purpose of Matthew's Gospel: Matthean Scholarship from 1945–1980." ANRW II. 25. 3. Berlin: Walter de Gruyter, 1983. More generally, see John K. Riches, *A Century of New Testament Study* (Harrisburg, Pa.: Trinity Press International, 1993).

3. "Additional Preparation Exercise" for leader, facilitator, and scribes is given at the end of this chapter. It invites you (and other participants if they wish) to compare your interpretation with Augustine's interpretation of the Beatitudes.

4. To recognize the specificity of our own interpretation, prior to the discussion, compare the contextual choices of your interpretation with those of Augustine. Saint Augustine, Bishop of Hippo, *The Preaching of Augustine;* Augustine: *"Our Lord's Sermon on the Mount,"* ed. Jaroslav Pelikan, trans. Francine Cardman (Philadelphia: Fortress Press, 1973). (Altered for inclusive vocabulary.)

CHAPTER 2

The Beatitudes in Scholarly Research and Popular Culture: Matthew 5:3-12

This chapter follows the pattern of the preceding one. After an introduction that provides a guide and tools for a second roundtable, it invites you to (1) prepare for a second roundtable on the beatitudes, (2) hold a second roundtable with a group, and (3) share its results.

Introduction: Goals of a Second Roundtable on a Bible Passage

Adding Participants to the Roundtable

Our starting point is the observation that there are many interpretations of every biblical passage. The contextual interpretations prepared by group members for the first roundtable (see chapter 1) are examples of one sort of interpretation: scriptural interpretations that deliberately look for the teaching of the Bible passage for believers and their lives in particular contexts. There are many other quite different kinds of interpretations: for example, sermons (or sermonlike interpretations), theological interpretations, and analytical interpretations (also called exegesis). What kinds of interpretations should be welcome at the Bible study group's roundtable? As this chapter will make clear, it is greatly beneficial to welcome every kind of interpretation into the conversation. This is a necessary part of scriptural criticism, a way for us to look at our contextual, scriptural interpretations from a distance and to have a clearer view of their characteristics.

This chapter focuses on the contributions of four kinds of professional interpreters' biblical scholars, theologians, and preachers, as well as gifted laypersons such as novelists and poets. First, however, it is necessary to make clear that the ground rules for the roundtable have not changed: (a) Everyone sitting around this table has equal rights and authority; (b) everyone is expected to make a genuine contribution, that is, to bring something different to the group's understanding of the richness of the biblical text; and (c) the goal of the discussion is to appreciate the distinctive contribution of each interpretation.

But how is this possible? Do interpretations not differ so greatly that they are truly incomparable? Do not certain interpretations—those of the scholars—have more authority than others? The answer for the contextual approach is that beyond their differences, these different kinds of interpretations are comparable and each interpreter has something to contribute to the discussion. Therefore, each interpretation has a special kind of authority at the roundtable. It will be important for the discussion that follows to distinguish the contribution of each interpreter. What then are the differences among the interpretations of novelists and poets, preachers, theologians, and biblical scholars? Most generally, these interpretations differ because the people who formulated them have different concerns.

Laypersons and preachers are primarily concerned with relating the Bible text directly to the needs of believers in a particular context; their primary interest is the teaching of the text for believers. In the preceding contextual exercise (roundtable 1), we chose to read the Bible in terms of a particular context in which believers have specific needs or problems, much as a preacher would. In each instance, you made a contextual choice.

Theologians emphasize another kind of choice in their theological interpretations. When they formulate their interpretations, they are eager to learn what the text has to say about certain theological concepts and issues (for example, about God, Christ, salvation, or discipleship). Since any Bible passage may refer to several theological concepts, each theological interpretation reflects a particular theological choice.

Similarly, biblical scholars make a different kind of choice when they are engaged in their technical analysis of the Bible text (often called exegesis). Each of their interpretations reflects a particular textual choice. With this choice, the biblical scholar selects certain features of the text as most significant.

You already know what contextual choices are. Preparing for a first roundtable involved becoming aware of contextual choices. The exercise required that each of you select one teaching of the beatitudes, rather than another, because that teaching addressed the needs of believers in a particular context. In the process you had to decide to which life contexts the beatitudes were relevant and to choose the life context that appeared to be particularly appropriate. Conversely, you implicitly decided that the beatitudes are less relevant for other life contexts in which believers may find themselves. In other words, you did not force the text to address every situation. Rather than "reading into the text" a teaching for believers in a situation that, in your view, the beatitudes do not address, you decided to choose another context. Seeking the best possible fit between context and Bible passage is making a contextual choice. And you did not make this choice lightly. You envisioned the theological convictions of the Christians in this context and you carefully considered the features of the biblical text (referring to certain verses and phrases). Thus, as members of the Bible study group, you have already demonstrated that a believer's sermonlike contextual interpretation must:

1. give more weight to those theological concepts in a Bible passage that are most closely associated with the teaching that believers need—therefore, implicitly or explicitly, contextual interpretation also includes a *theological choice*—and
2. give more weight to those textual features of the Bible passage that are most significant because they express the particular teaching that believers need in their life context—therefore, implicitly or explicitly, contextual interpretation also includes a *textual choice*.

In a sermon (or layperson's interpretation), the most apparent interpretive choice is most often contextual, but the interpretation also involves theological and textual choices, even though these are less apparent. The same is true for the other types of interpretations. In a theological interpretation, the most apparent interpretive choice is theological, but it also involves less apparent contextual and textual choices. A biblical scholar's interpretation (or exegesis) most obviously involves textual choices, but it also involves theological and contextual choices.[1]

Identifying the interpretive choices that are most apparent in different types of interpretations is useful, but not sufficient. These distinctions alone do not provide a critical perspective on the great variety of interpretations of the Gospel of Matthew or any other Bible passage. By themselves, these distinctions may allow readers to dismiss as meaningless or unhelpful the kinds of interpretations they do not practice themselves. Thus, biblical scholars may ignore the insights of sermons and theological interpretations; theologians may view exegetical studies and sermons as marginal; and preachers and laypeople may attend only to sermons. On the other hand, acknowledging that any interpretation of the Bible involves these three types of interpretive choices should encourage a more respectful attitude toward all kinds of interpretations. Whether or not a given interpretation makes it explicit, the interpreter or artist has made contextual, theological, and textual choices that can be compared with the contextual, theological, and textual choices of any other interpretation of the same Bible passage.

Then, everyone around the table, whether they bring a sermon, a theological interpretation, a poetic interpretation, or a scholarly biblical exegesis, has something to contribute to the discussion and should be treated with equal respect. She or he has paid greatest attention to one of the three interpretive choices and deserves to be heard by everyone who is interested enough by this text to read it and propose an interpretation of it.

Gaining a Critical Perspective on the Many Interpretations of the Biblical Text

From the preceding section, it is clear that no interpretation, including the so-called "results of biblical scholarship," is the benchmark against which all other interpretations should be assessed. This will be puzzling to some. As noted already, the concern of this approach is to avoid dismissing as worthless, or reducing to the rank of voiceless subordinates, all the interpretations that explicitly or implicitly use different benchmarks—for instance, those chosen by interpreters of different cultures or subcultures or of different social groups or of different religious backgrounds.

Some may ask: If there are several culturally marked benchmarks, does this mean that for each biblical text there is more than one legitimate interpretation? The answer is an unequivocal yes.

Then, does this mean that critical biblical studies are useless? Of course, not! On the contrary, a critical perspective on the many interpretations of the Gospel of Matthew is desirable. It helps us better understand this Gospel and its wealth of potential teachings. Thus, far from ignoring the "results" of critical biblical scholarship, it is important to take note of the diversity of these results.

Biblical scholars reach diverse conclusions regarding the Gospel of Matthew (or any other biblical text). Why? Because they use different critical approaches in their efforts to seek to correct three kinds of problems they find with too many interpretations of the Bible. The three problems biblical scholars are concerned with are related to the three kinds of interpretive choices we have already named (although the order of priority for biblical scholars has been different):

(a) Textual problems: Claims that cannot be supported by the text and thus betray the text; the "most significant textual features" need to exist!

(b) Theological problems: Dangerous and destructive theologies and religious convictions.

(c) Contextual problems: Oppressive uses of the Bible within a particular context, uses that are hurtful and unjust or condone hurtful behaviors and social systems.

You may think that the existence of a plurality of interpretations in the group is the problem that needs to be overcome with the help of critical biblical scholarship—that should then establish the only and universally true interpretation. But, as we already suggested, the primary problem that Bible study groups have to confront is the opposite one. Claiming that there is only one true meaning of a Bible passage is the most frequent and tenacious problem—and a betrayal of the Bible. A single, absolutely true interpretation does not exist, despite the claims of historicist scholars who seek to establish the so-called objective meaning of the text and those of fundamentalist Christians who read the text for its so-called literal meaning. Such claims are betrayals of the text because each biblical passage is a discourse, whose meaning is, and has always been, incarnated in the way the text affects its readers. Ordinary believers are right when they recognize Bible passages as "living words" through which they discern particular "words to live by" that vary according to the contexts of their lives.

Consequently, interpretations that cannot be supported by a Bible text (and thus betray this text) include not only those that misread some parts of the text (for example, confusing one word for another), but also interpretations that aim at establishing the single true meaning of the Bible text. It also follows that people are misguided when they expect, as many do, that an expert (a biblical scholar, a historian, a preacher) will teach us the true (single) meaning of the text.

What, then, is the role of a teacher or Bible study leader in the second roundtable? To begin with, we can say most clearly what it is not: It is not to read the text for you, not to tell you what it means, and not to show you how it applies to the lives of believers today. No teacher can present to students the one true interpretation because it does not reside with the teacher. Such an absolute, true interpretation does not exist. The role of the teacher or Bible study leader in the second roundtable is threefold:

The leader's first role is to help members of the groups discover what they already know. Even if they are reading the New Testament for the first time, they know how to discern what the Bible is teaching believers in a particular context.

The leader's second role is to facilitate roundtable discussions, by making sure that the group appreciates the contribution of each person around the table, that is, appreciates what is *different* in the proposed contextual interpretation of each. These first two roles were also important for the first roundtable, but they are ongoing roles. All of the members of a group, not just the teacher, should be encouraged to exercise this role vis-à-vis the other members of the group during the roundtable discussions.

The leader's third role is to help members of the group gain a critical perspective on the diverse readings of the assigned passage of the Gospel of Matthew. As biblical scholars, teachers are "experts" in two senses: (a) they know many interpretations of each text, and (b) they have been trained to use critical methods.

a) They are aware of the existence of many different interpretations of any Bible passage through a knowledge of the history of biblical interpretation. With this awareness, it becomes most difficult to claim that there is only one true interpretation—which just happens to be mine! Seen in this light, the claim to know the one true interpretation of a Bible passage would appear the height of arrogance. Thus, to help the members of the group gain a first critical distance from their respective interpretations, the teacher provides many interpretations for each passage to be discussed in the second roundtable. Thus, this book provides a sampling of such interpretations for each passage of the Gospel of Matthew to be discussed.

b) Teachers have been trained to identify the characteristics of each interpretation, so that differing interpretations may be appropriately compared with one another. One efficient way to compare interpretations is to do so in terms of the three kinds of interpretive choices: contextual, theological, and textual.[2]

Comparing Interpretations in Terms of Their Theological *Choices*

To understand a biblical text is to enter into dialogue with it. In seeking understanding, we bring to the text our theological views—our conceptions of a believer's life under God. This is appropriate, since as a religious text the Bible deals with such issues. This is possible for any reader, including nonbelievers; our theological views remain theological even if they are negative ones.

As in any true dialogue, we must also expect that our own views will be somehow altered and radically transformed. As you enter in dialogue with a Bible passage, you inevitably bring with you your own views of Scripture. You choose, as we already discussed during the first roundtable, to view the text as something akin to a "lamp to my feet," "canon," "book of the covenant or family album," the "good news," "corrective glasses," "empowering Word," or "Holy Bible." This is a first general theological choice. It is a choice that, even if you are not a Christian believer yourself, you spontaneously make as soon as you think about a passage of the Gospel of Matthew as one with teachings for the life of Christian believers.

Furthermore, as with any dialogue, conversation with the assigned Bible passage involves finding an issue, topic, or subject matter in which both the interpreter and the text are interested. In an actual dialogue, the partners have different knowledge levels about the chosen topic; one may be much more knowledgeable than the other. Thus, at first, the dialogue partners seek to ascertain the level of knowledge and the perspective of the other on the topic. Then, as they begin to know and trust each other, truly intersubjective, reciprocal, heart-to-heart exchanges take place. When such a true dialogue fully unfolds, whether or not the two partners agree, they understand each other on the subject matter. Truly understanding the other calls for a continuation of the dialogue because one is aware that there is always more to know about the other's perspective.

So it is with your dialogue with a Bible text. At first, you must learn about the text and its views on the topic and ascertain the extent to which you can trust the text on this subject matter. Then, your dialogue with the Bible passage may become intersubjective and reciprocal. Beyond a simple awareness of what the text says about the topic, you become aware of the particular perspective the Bible passage has on the chosen topic and how the Bible passage brings to light your particular way of looking at this topic. In other words, the interpreter reads the text and the text reads the interpreter, so much so that the interpreter also perceives her or his own view of the topic from the perspective of the text.

Understanding a biblical text—especially when it is read as Scripture—involves a respect for its mystery, the expectation that it will surprise us and challenge our views. It also involves being confident that the Bible passage will welcome us as persons with our own ever-changing views and perspectives. Then, respecting the mystery of a biblical text means that each time we read it we must make sense of it anew because the subject matter of our reading is in constant flux.

The role of the interpreter's theological choices is best understood by taking a concrete example: our interpretations of the beatitudes during the first roundtable. We led you to frame your interpretation in terms of particular theological concepts by asking, "What is the teaching of Matthew 5:3-12 'for Christians and their lives as disciples today'?" Thus, you implicitly or explicitly entered in dialogue with the text regarding the theological concept of "discipleship." Your dialogue with the text about discipleship can best be represented by twin questions:

- How did you conceive of discipleship? What concept of discipleship did you bring to the text? What did you want to know about discipleship, with the expectation that the text would have something to say about it?
- What did you learn from the text about discipleship? That is, what was new for you about discipleship in the text? On which issue did the text surprise you by expressing something totally unexpected?

The same kind of questions needs to be raised about any subject matter, especially any theological theme, about which readers enter into dialogue with a Bible text. Of course, for true dialogue, the text must have something to say about this concept, theme, or issue. This is what any reader verifies by paying close attention to the text and by identifying—making a textual choice of—the features of the text that will be "most significant."

Comparing Interpretations in Terms of Their Textual *Choices*

Any given biblical passage can be analyzed using a broad range of critical exegetical methods, each of which views certain features of the text as most significant. Any biblical passage has several significant features, and every interpretation implicitly or explicitly makes a textual choice by focusing on certain features viewed as most significant.

This point is readily illustrated by considering a simpler and different kind of text—the following black and white cognitive test diagram. When we perceive the vase (candlestick), our attention is focused on the white features of the drawing. Our focus on the white vase momentarily hides from our perception the two faces (persons) looking at each other, which are nevertheless represented by the same image. And conversely, we only see the two faces when we focus our attention on the black features.

Biblical texts are like this diagram in the sense that they have several different significant features. Each time we read a biblical text, we choose a certain set of features as most significant and ignore the significance of the other sets of features. In biblical studies, this has become more visible with the increasing diversification of methods. (See the chart Bible Study Methods and the Textual Features They Emphasize).

Three kinds of textual features are commonly taken as "most significant": those that point to a world behind the text; those that point to a world within the text; and those that point to a world in front of the text.

1) Behind the Text. For quite a number of analytical methods—in this case, those usually referred to as exegetical methods—the most significant textual features are those that point to something behind the text:

- A person (for example, Jesus or Matthew) and his teaching to a particular audience (such as, the crowds in Galilee or early Christians for whom Matthew wrote)
- The author's intention. For example, what did Jesus seek to achieve by his teaching in parables, or what are the misunderstandings in the church in Syria that Matthew intended to correct by writing his Gospel?
- An institution (for example, the church in Matthew's day)
- A religious situation (for example, the different Jewish groups in Jesus' day or the relationship between the synagogue and the church in Matthew's day)
- A social, economic, or political reality (for example, the complex reality of the Roman Empire)

In order to further explain what is behind the text, biblical scholars use historical criticism (including sociological, economic, political, and cultural criticisms; history of religions; source criticism; form criticism; redaction criticism; or any number of historical exegetical methods; see the chart "Bible Study Methods and the Textual Features They Emphasize" on pp. 54-57).

2) Within the Text. For quite a number of analytical methods—those usually referred to as literary methods—the text's most significant features are its literary characteristics:

- The unfolding of the narrative plot. For example, in Matthew, this could include the unfolding of Jesus' story from genealogy and birth to crucifixion and resurrection, or the story of the disciples from their call (Matt. 4:18-22) to their final commissioning (Matt. 28:16-20).
- The construction of narrative characters. For example, how Jesus or the disciples are developed as complex characters in the narrative of Matthew.
- The construction of symbolic figures and metaphors, implying a compari-

son with another text or tradition. For example, Matthew portrays Jesus as a Moses-like figure. For Matthew, Jesus is a new Moses who goes up on the mountain and gives, from there, new teachings about the Law (see Matt. 5:21-48) to the new people of God. These actions of Jesus are portrayed in ways reminiscent of those performed by Moses in Exodus 19–20.

- The figurative organization of the text. That there are nine beatitudes (or three groups of three) or that the Lord's Prayer is at the very center of the Sermon on the Mount represents such figurative organization.
- Structural characteristics of the text. For example, why was the confrontation between Jesus and the Canaanite woman presented as a confrontation, rather than as a friendly encounter? The relationship between beginning and ending of the Sermon on the Mount, with the sharp contrast between the beatitudes (blessings) and the judgment scenes (condemnations), are also significant structural characteristics.

In order to explain what is in the text, a biblical scholar may use one of the literary methods (textual, literary, narrative, or structural criticism; see the chart Bible Study Methods and the Textual Features They Emphasize).

3) **In Front of the Text.** For quite a number of other analytical methods the most significant features of a text are those that signal how the text, as a discourse, affects its hearers or readers and the situations in which they find themselves. Here, the most significant textual features are those that transform a reader's behavior or view of reality, or that more directly address (affirm, reject, or seek to transform) the social, economic, or political realities of the readers' situations:

- Rhetorical features of the text. Examples of significant rhetorical features are Paul's exclamation of rebuking the Corinthians (1 Cor. 14:36) and Jesus' claim of authority over the readers, who are expected to acknowledge this authority as the crowds did (see Matt. 5–7).
- Textual features that highlight what is presupposed and thus condoned, advocated, or rejected regarding social, economic, political, and religious structures of authority. For example, the text may exhibit traces of an androcentric perspective, by which women's points of view are excluded and ignored. The text may exhibit traces of patriarchal structures, often presupposed by New Testament texts, and also, at times, challenged by them. When such presuppositions are challenged, they are often represented in the text with a "twist," such as when some texts present God the Father with motherlike attributes. The text may also challenge social and economic injustice, such as when the Greek *dikaiosyne* is translated "justice" instead of "righteousness" in the beatitudes; or the text may challenge imperial polit-

ical structure by using the word "kingdom"—commonly used to designate the Roman Empire—to refer to God's empire.
- Mention of marginalized people in the text, which allows the readers to envision a different social and cultural construction of reality. For example, the mention of people who are poor in spirit, mourning, meek, or hungry and thirsty for justice may be significant in that it allows readers to imagine themselves anew. They are encouraged to see themselves as citizens of a kingdom in which they will be comforted, no longer deprived from the land, and satisfied with the justice they once lacked (Matt. 5:3-5).

In order to focus on one or another thing in front of the text, a biblical scholar may use a reader-centered method—such as reader-response, feminist, or postcolonial criticism (including reader-centered political and cultural criticisms)—and the highlighting of voices from the margin (see the chart Bible Study Methods and the Textual Features They Emphasize).

In sum, each interpreter has necessarily made a certain textual choice. The interpreter has chosen a certain kind of textual feature as most significant. We first distinguish interpretations by their respective choices regarding the location of what is most significant: Is it what is behind the text, within the text, or in front of the text? We then look more closely at the most significant textual features for each given interpretation.

Scholars now often make such textual choices explicit in biblical studies. Such studies usually include a section that specifies the methods used and underscores the specific focus of the study on certain textual features. When pastors formulate their sermons (contextual interpretations), and when theologians formulate their theological interpretations, they also determine for themselves what features are most significant (even if only provisionally significant). However, pastors and theologians do not often make their textual choices explicit. Nevertheless, they have made them. In order to compare the interpretations of pastors and theologians (or artists or storytellers) with those of biblical scholars, we need to tease out of sermons and theological interpretations and paintings and stories the textual choices that the interpreters have made. The following chart, "Bible Study Methods and the Textual Features They Emphasize," summarizes the type of questions each method addresses to the text and the kind of significant textual features with which each is primarily concerned. During the last century, a growing number of methods in the humanities and social sciences were adopted in biblical studies. Here is a list of methods and what each defines as most significant in the text by the questions they ask.

Bible Study Methods and the Textual Features They Emphasize

HISTORICAL METHOD	TO WHAT DOES THE TEXT AS WINDOW REFER?	WHAT IS MOST SIGNIFICANT "BEHIND THE TEXT"?
Historical criticism and history-centered versions of textual, sociological, economic, political, cultural, and ideological criticisms and history of religions	• Who wrote the text? When? Why was it written? What is the life setting of the writer and of the intended readers? To what historical events or persons does the text refer? • What are the social, economic, political, cultural, and religious settings of the biblical book? How are they reflected in the text? How does the text address them?	• The intention of the author (what the author meant), significant because of the author's authority. • Historical events (for example, Jesus' ministry and passion) and persons to whom the text refers (Jesus, Paul, Peter); significant as are the foundation of the Christian faith. • The way the text addresses social, economic, political, cultural, or religious issues of that time; significant because it shows how the text can address similar or different situations today.
Source criticism	• Can we detect the use of written sources in this text (such as the use of Mark and the source Q by Matthew and Luke, or of traditional material in Paul's letters)? What are these sources?	• Identified written sources are most significant because they give us access to the teaching of the earliest church, bringing us closer to Jesus.
Form criticism	• Can we detect the use of oral traditions by the "forms" that reflect their "settings in life" (e.g., their oral use in missionary activity, in preaching, in instruction of new converts, in baptism or the Lord's Supper)?	• Identified oral traditions used in the New Testament are most significant because they give us access to the liturgical practice of the earliest church, bringing us closer to Jesus.
Redaction criticism	• Can we detect the characteristic ways in which the author has edited or "redacted" written sources and oral traditions to compose the text? Missions, changes, or additions that Matthew made when using Mark? When using source Q? When using oral traditions? • Can we recognize the writer's point of view in the way the text is "redacted"? The particular theological perspective of the author?	• The distinctive theological point of view of the author or editor (redactor) of each book of the New Testament is most significant because of the author's authority.

LITERARY METHOD	WHAT IS THE TEXT? HOW CAN IT BE DESCRIBED?	WHAT IS MOST SIGNIFICANT "WITHIN THE TEXT"?
Textual criticism	• Among the existing handwritten manuscripts, what is the oldest? Why are variants (differences) found in later manuscripts? Are they simple mechanical copying errors? • Do variants reflect theological or political controversies and views?	• The older text is most significant (because closer to the original). • Variants can be viewed as significant readings.
Literary criticism and its extension in history of traditions, history of religions, and literary conception of redactioncriticism	• What is the genre of the text or of one of its parts? What is a parable? Is a Gospel a biography? An ancient history? A kerygmatic (sermonlike) work? Or does it belong to some other Jewish or Hellenistic literary genre? How are Paul's letters related to the Hellenistic epistolary genre? • What is the style of the work? Its symbolism? How does it use figurative language? • To which other texts or traditions or religious views does the work allude to construct figures (such as "Jesus as Moses-like")?	• The symbolic world constructed by the text is most significant because it provides a vision that the readers are invited to enter and share. • The symbolic message of the text.
Narrative criticism	• Regarding the explicit story presented in a Gospel or the story implied by a letter: Who are the characters? How do they relate to one another? How does the plot unfold in one or several story lines? How are characters and situations transformed through the unfolding of the plot?	• Most significant are those characters with whom readers can identify—Jesus, the disciples, the women, Paul, his addressees—and the unfolding of the stories (plot) of these characters because they become the stories of the readers who identify with them.
Structural criticism	• What is the pattern (or structure) of transformation marked in the text? How does the ending of a book (or of one of its passages) reflect a transformation of the situation presented at the beginning? How is this structural transformation clarified by the contrasts highlighted by the conflicts between characters in the story or by other polemical features of the text?	• Most significant are the basic convictions—self-evident views, the core of faith—posited by the text, presupposed and held by the author, and offered to readers. Readers are invited to share these basic convictions by entering the narrative or discourse.

RHETORICAL AND IDEOLOGICAL METHOD	HOW DOES THE TEXT AFFECT ITS READERS?	WHAT IS MOST SIGNIFICANT "IN FRONT OF THE TEXT"?
Rhetorical criticism	• To whom is this addressed? The hoped-for effect upon the readers? The author's strategy in appealing to the readers? What kind of persuasion does it employ? To make a judgment about past events (judical, or legal, rhetoric)? Does the author seek to persuade the readers to take some action in the future (deliberative, or political, rhetoric)? To celebrate or denounce some person or lifestyle (epideictic, or ceremonial, rhetoric)?	• The effect that the author intended the work to have as discourse upon the readers or hearers in the past is most significant, either because con-temporary readers need to be affected in the same way, or because this intended effect does not apply in the present situation.
Reader-response criticism	• How are real readers in particular situations affected by the Bible pas-sage? What is particularly significant for them in the text? How do they use the text? How are readers helped or hurt by the text? How are they affected by the text?	• The different kinds of features through which the Bible passage affects readers are the most significant, whether these features and their effects on readers are intentional on the part of the author or not.
Feminist criticism	• How are female characters portrayed in the text? Is there an androcen-tric (male-centered) bias? How does this bias limit the women's abilities and roles in society? Is there a patriarchal bias, through which women are subordinated to men? Can we detect a reaction against such biases in the text?	• The features through which this text affects and has affected women are the most significant. These include the features of the Bible text that have a detrimental and oppressive effect upon women, as well as those that have a constructive and liberationist effect for women.

Postcolonial criticism and reader-centered versions of sociological, economic, political, cultural, and ideological criticisms	• What are the power/authority structures—political or not—represented by the Bible passage? How is the status of different people indicated and valued? How are people of other cultures represented? Who are despised? Marginalized? Excluded? In power? Who "lord over" others? • How are readers affected by of sociological, economic, political, and cultural realities?	• The views of power and authority, of oppression, of exclusion, of colonialism that are in the text and conveyed by the text are the most significant. • Signs of resistance against such power and strategies of resistance are also most significant.
Intertextual reading Intercontextual reading	• Reading a text in terms of—and from the perspective of—another text. When the intertext (passage related to the text for comparison or contrast) is from the Bible, this is called "canonical criticism." • Intercontextual: A reading of the text from the perspective of a present-day context. In both cases, one asks: • How does a person receive the biblical text from that other perspective? What does one perceive in the text that was invisible without the intertext?	• Most significant are the similarities and differences between the biblical text and the related text (intertext) or context (intercontext). • What is brought to light in the text when looking at it from the perspective of the inter-text or intercontext.
Voices from the Margin	• Whose presence is acknowledged in the text, even though they are simply alluded to and remain silent? How does recognizing their presence affect readers who are presently marginalized or who empathize with the marginalized? • Reading the text from the perspective of present-day marginalized people.	• The most significant is the perception that one has of the action, the situation, the main characters, and the central teaching when one considers them from the perspective of the marginalized characters. The cries one hears when listening to these "voices from the margins."

I—Preparing for a Second Roundtable on the Beatitudes (Matt. 5:3-12)

For this second roundtable, we invite other interpreters of the beatitudes: W. D. Davies and Dale C. Allison Jr., two biblical scholars; Alice Walker, a novelist; Clarence Jordan, a pastor; and Georg Strecker, a biblical scholar. Do not be intimidated. Like yours, each of their interpretations makes interpretive choices. Your task is to compare the choices you have made with the choices of these interpreters. To assist in this task, we present a comparison of their respective contextual choices, theological choices (including their specific views of Scripture and discipleship), and textual choices.

We do not claim to present the "only true" characteristics of these interpretations, but rather the characteristics of these interpretations that appear when we compare them with one another. As always, the point of our presentation is to clarify the differences among these four interpretations. (In addition, we implicitly noted differences with our own interpretations; see chapter 6.) If we compared one of these interpretations with another set of interpretations, we would necessarily have underscored different characteristics of its interpretive choices.

Similarly, you are invited to compare your own interpretive choices with these interpretations. You have already identified (in the first roundtable) some characteristics of your own contextual choices and one of your theological choices—the role you ascribed to Scripture. As you compare your own interpretations with these, you are now in a position to identify other characteristics of your interpretive choices, namely, characteristics of another of your theological choices—the view of discipleship you brought to the text—and of your textual choices. Regarding each of these choices, simply ask yourself: Which of these four interpretations are based on choices that are most similar to mine? (You might find that none of these are similar to yours.) How do these choices differ from mine? This is what you will want to discuss with the other members of your group during your second roundtable.[3]

1. W. D. Davies and Dale C. Allison Jr.: The Gospel According to Saint Matthew[4]

The Teaching of the Beatitudes for Believers According to Davies and Allison

Davies and Allison, together with most biblical scholars, do not make explicit the "teaching for believers" in their multivolume critical commentary on the Gospel of Matthew. Yet, as is the case with any scholarly study, their interpretation leans toward, and implicitly chooses, a particular view of the teaching of the text for believers. In the conclusion of their study of Matthew 5:3-12, Davies and Allison underscore five characteristics of the beatitudes that are readily comparable to the teachings for believers formulated by preachers and members of your roundtable.

The beatitudes bring a blessing from God: "The beatitudes are first of all blessings, not requirements. So by opening the sermon on the mount they place it within the context of grace. . . . The hard commands of Matthew 5–7 presuppose God's mercy and prior saving activity."[5]

The beatitudes promise the kingdom: "The kingdom of God will bring eschatological comfort, a permanent inheritance, true satisfaction, the obtaining of mercy, the vision of God [and the recognition that one is a child of God]. . . . The word 'kingdom' serves to foretell the eventual realization in human experience of the fullness of God's bounteous presence."[6]

The beatitudes reveal who Jesus is: In Isaiah 61:1-3, "the person who brings good tidings to the poor and comforts those in mourning is an anointed one and bearer of the Spirit. . . . He is the Messiah."[7]

The beatitudes call disciples to imitate Jesus because "the beatitudes are illustrated and brought to life by Jesus' actions": "Jesus was himself meek (11:29; 21:5). Jesus mourned (26:36-46). Jesus was righteous and 'fulfilled all righteousness' (3:15; 27:4, 19). Jesus showed mercy (9:27; 15:22; 17:15; 20:30-31). And Jesus was persecuted and reproached (26-27)."[8]

The beatitudes give "a secret vision and hope that makes powerlessness and suffering bearable": they "lessen pain and anguish and effect encouragement (cf. 10:26-30) . . . through an exercise of the imagination (cf. on 9:12). Eschatological promises for the poor, the meek, and the persecuted reveal that all is not what it seems to be."[9]

Davies and Allison's Interpretive Choices

What are the interpretive choices that led Davies and Allison to these conclusions? As biblical scholars, they emphasize their textual choices. So let us begin with these.

Textual Choices

> *Most Significant Textual Features:* **"within the text"**; figurative and symbolic message; style; allusions to the Septuagint (or LXX, the Old Testament in Greek) and to Jewish traditions; and parallels with other religious texts (including other New Testament texts).
>
> *Methods:* literary criticism, with history of traditions and (literary form of) redaction criticism.

Davies and Allison reach their conclusions regarding the teaching of the beatitudes because for them the most significant features are those highlighted when one reads them in terms of both (1) the rest of the Gospel of Matthew, with special attention to its literary style and organization, and (2) the passages of the Septuagint (Greek translation of the Hebrew Bible) and of Jewish traditions to which the beatitudes allude. Their approach is historical, but in an "eclectic" way, with an emphasis on the history of traditions.[10] In contrast with Strecker (below), who clearly focuses on what is behind the text, Davies and Allison focus on what is in the text. In this way, Davies and Allison underscore the figurative and symbolic features of the beatitudes (Jesus as Moses-like and Messiah). Thus, for them, the beatitudes are proclamations by Jesus, the Messiah, who is both like the one who brings good tidings in Isaiah 61:1-2 and like Moses on *Mount* Sinai.[11] These proclamations are given to disciples who are like the blessed ones in the Psalms and the prophets.[12] The beatitudes concern the rule/kingdom of God and its economy which are unlike foreign or false rules/kingdoms and their economies. Thus, Davies and Allison give a detailed list of the biblical texts to which each of the beatitudes alludes. For instance, the references in Matthew 5:3 to the "poor" is interpreted as people who are in a state of "economic poverty" (Prov. 13:8) or who see themselves in special need of God's help (Ps. 12:5, 14:6, 22:24; and Isaiah 61:1; and in many early Jewish texts including the Dead Sea Scrolls). Being "poor in spirit" does not mean becoming humble, but recognizing that one needs God's help because of one's economic poverty.

1) Reading the Beatitudes as Part of a Literary Work: The Gospel of Matthew. The beatitudes as a Proclamation by Jesus, the Messiah, a Moses-like Teacher of Israel. For Davies and Allison, it is significant that Matthew 5:3-12 (the beatitudes) is the introduction to the Sermon on the Mount, which is itself the first of the five discourses in Matthew: chapters 5–7, 10, 13, 18, and 23–25. As there are five books of Moses (Genesis, Exodus, Leviticus, Numbers, and Deuteronomy), there are five discourses by Jesus. Jesus also fulfills prophecies, presented as "formula citations" (introduced by words such as "this was to fulfill what had been spoken by the Lord through the prophet"), in Matthew 1:22, 2:15, 2:17, 2:23, 4:14, 8:17, 12:17, 13:35, 21:4, and 27:9. In the Sermon on the Mount, Moses fulfills the "law and the prophets" (Matt. 5:17). Thus, Davies and Allison find it most significant that "Matthew 1–5 in all its parts reflects an exodus typology":[13] What happened in the time of the Hebrew Bible exodus happens again in the time of Jesus and thus "fulfills" the type of the exodus. Davies and Allison explain: "The gospel opens with events recalling the birth and childhood of Moses (Matt. 2:13-21). Then there is Jesus' baptism, which parallels Israel passing through the waters (Matt.

3:13-17). There follows next the temptation (Matt. 4:1-11), in which Jesus re-experiences the desert temptations recounted in Deuteronomy. Finally, there is Matthew 4:23–5:2, where Jesus, like Moses, sits on the mountain of revelation. . . . He is speaking as the mosaic Messiah and delivering messianic Torah."[14]

The constant allusions to biblical texts (including also the Psalms and the prophets) in the beatitudes and the rest of the Sermon on the Mount show that Jesus' teaching, which he embodies in his ministry, is in continuity with the Bible and the Jewish traditions it fulfills. Further, it is also superior to that of the scribes and Pharisees (Matt. 5:17-20, as well as 7:29). Jesus is both like Moses and unlike Moses. The figurative style of the Gospel of Matthew, written in the last decade of the first century, underscores its polemic against the Pharisees, who are called "hypocrites." This polemic is not anti-Jewish (or anti-Semitic); rather, it reflects an inter-Jewish conflict between Jewish Pharisees and the Jewish followers of Jesus.

Davies and Allison also pay attention to the way in which Matthew used his sources, including the Gospel of Mark and of the source Q (from German, Quelle; meaning source, a collection of sayings of Jesus, also used by Luke). Thus, they used redaction criticism. But, by contrast with Strecker, they do so with a literary focus that pays special attention to the ways in which Matthew amplified the allusions to the Bible (LXX) and Jewish traditions, and thus made a figurative presentation of Jesus and his teaching (for example, Jesus as Moses-like). Such a figurative presentation imparted to Matthew's church the vision it needed in order to have a proper understanding of discipleship, understood as imitating Jesus.

2) The Beatitudes in the Sermon on the Mount. Since Jesus' Moses-like teaching is in continuity with biblical and Jewish teachings, the opening of the Sermon on the Mount, the beatitudes, is like the opening of the law given on Mount Sinai. As Exodus 20 first presents what God has done for Israel (vv. 1-2) before presenting the law (vv. 3ff.), so the beatitudes introduce the teaching about the law by referring to the blessings brought by God and God's saving activity both in the present and in the coming kingdom. They provide a vision of "the eventual realization in human experience of the fullness of God's bounteous presence" a vision of the kingdom.[15]

Theological Choices

> *Role of the Text as Scripture*: Book of the Covenant (Testament) Family Album.
>
> *View of Discipleship:* Sharing in the vision of the kingdom and imitating Jesus (who embodies his teaching and the kingdom).
>
> *View of the Moral Life:* Perfectionist.

Since this interpretation underscores the vision offered by the beatitudes, it presupposes one of the three roles of Scripture that relate to faith and vision: Book of the Covenant or Family Album, Corrective Glasses, or Holy Bible (see pp. 27-28). To a certain extent, the beatitudes shatter the believers' views of the world (the role of the Holy Bible) and give a vision of what God is doing in the believers' lives (the role of Scripture as corrective glasses). But for Davies and Allison, the essential role of the beatitudes is to give its readers a sense that they are children of God (Matt. 5:9) and belong, with Jesus, to the family of God. Thus the primary role of Scripture for Davies and Allison is Book of the Covenant or Family Album.

Clear from Davies and Allison's conclusions is that they understand discipleship as imitating Christ. As Christ embodied the teaching of the beatitudes (by being meek and so on), so should his disciples. For this, the disciples must see (have the vision of) Jesus as a model to be imitated. Jesus manifests the kingdom and thus reveals life in the kingdom. Discipleship begins with sharing the symbolic world offered by the beatitudes, a vision of the eschatological kingdom of complete obedience and holiness as a fulfillment of Jewish traditions and expectations. Discipleship is striving toward this perfection, imitating Jesus. This is following a perfectionist view of the moral life, according to which a good moral life is gained by imitating a virtuous person (here, Jesus) and progressively growing in virtue toward perfection. It is acquiring virtues by imitating the expert (Christ), as an apprentice does.

Contextual Choices

Problem in the Interpreters' Life Context: European Americans in a post-holocaust setting; concerns for the relationship between Christianity and Judaism.
Root Problem: Lack of faith/vision of the kingdom.

As biblical scholars, Davies and Allison claim "to be loyal to the tradition of disinterested and objective study in biblical criticism," a claim with which we disagree (as already noted).[16] Accordingly, they emphasize the textual dimension of interpretation and do not make explicit either the teaching of the beatitudes for believers today or their concern for a particular contextual problem. Yet, when we compare their interpretation with the following ones by Alice Walker, Clarence Jordan, and Georg Strecker, the root problem that Davies and Allison's interpretation helps believers address becomes apparent: a lack of vision. For them (by contrast with Jordan), the beatitudes do not provide knowledge of God's will; they are "not requirements."[17] In fact, for Davies and Allison (by contrast with Strecker), believers should already know what they should do since most of the instructions of the Sermon on the Mount are already found in the Bible and in Jewish traditions. Furthermore, for them (by contrast with Walker), the beatitudes do not aim to empower people who lack ability or are powerless. Davies and Allison's interpretation does presuppose that believers are discouraged and need comfort or may lack the will to do what they should. However, for Davies and Allison, the root problem is clearly that believers lack faith or vision. The beatitudes give them a vision of God's grace and mercy, of the kingdom, of their place in its future. It is "a secret vision" that "all is not what it seems to be."[18] It is a vision of Jesus as the model to be imitated.

This vision is expressed in Jewish terms, emphasizing the continuity between Judaism and Christianity, and presenting the polemic of Matthew against the Pharisees as a dispute within the Jewish family—Matthew was "a Jew writing for Jews."[19] This emphasis suggests that Davies and Allison are concerned with anti-Jewish interpretations of Matthew. This becomes clear by comparisons with the interpretations by Walker, Jordan, and Strecker, for whom this is not a predominant concern.

2. Alice Walker, "The Gospel According to Shug" in *The Temple of My Familiar*[20]

The Teaching of the Beatitudes for Believers According to Walker

Helped are those who are enemies of their own racism: they shall live in harmony with the citizens of this world, and not with those of the world of their ancestors, which has passed away, and which they shall never see again.[21]

It is with this first beatitude that Alice Walker opens "The Gospel According to Shug." The readers have already encountered, in *The Color Purple*,[22] Shug and her "grandmother" Fanny—actually, the partner ("special friend") of her biological grandmother.[23] In the novel *The Temple of My Familiar*, the character Shug writes her "Gospel," a pamphlet that contains twenty-seven beatitudes. Shug understands the contextual character of interpretation, as she is quite weary of "the perverted interpretations of men."[24] This first of Shug's twenty-seven beatitudes is particularly important for Fanny because, together with other Africans and African Americans, she feels the white people's "oppression in every aspect of her existence." For Fanny, it is clear that "it's racism and greed that have to go. Not white people."[25] Yet twin questions remain unresolved: "But can they be separated from their racism?" And "Can I . . . maybe . . . stop racist oppression before it starts in myself?"[26] These questions are essential for Fanny, "one of those victims of racism who is extremely sensitive," because "racism turned her thoughts to violence. Violence made her sick. She was working on it."[27] Fanny is indeed an enemy of her own racism.

"Helped are those who *know*."[28] This, the last of Shug's twenty-seven beatitudes, puzzles other characters in the novel. Thus they ask: "know *what?*"[29] By asking this question, they discover that, in fact, they do not know. But what is it that they do not know? The readers of the novel are given a clue when Fanny explains that a church is for Shug a "prayer band," as "renegade black women's churches" were traditionally called. Shug's church is "a group of people who share a common bond and purpose and whose notion of the spiritual reality is radically at odds with mainstream of prevailing ones."[30] This spiritual reality that the members of the band "know" is expressed by the rest of the beatitudes in "The Gospel According to Shug" and is summarized[31] in the next to the last of Shug's beatitudes: "Helped are those who love and actively support the diversity of life; they shall be secure in their differentness."[32]

Others of Shug's beatitudes[33] are: Helped are "those who love the stranger"; "those who love others unsplit off from their faults"; "those who risk themselves for others' sakes"; "those whose every act is a prayer for peace"; "those who love all the colors of all the human beings . . . of animals and plants"; "those who love the lesbian, the gay, and the straight"; "those who love the broken and the whole"; "those who do not join mobs"; as well as "those who love" all other forms of life, creation, the universe; and thus "those who love the Earth, their mother, and who willingly suffer that she may not die."

The blessing "they shall be secure in their differentness" finds more concrete expression in the promises that "none of their children, nor any of their ancestors, nor any parts of themselves" shall be "hidden" or "despised"; that "they shall find mysteries so intriguing as to distract them from every blow"; and that the spirits of those who are called "illegitimate"—because they are "born from love: conceived in their father's tenderness and their mother's orgasm"—"shall know no boundaries, even between heaven and earth, and [their] eyes shall reveal the spark of the love that was their own creation."[34]

Walker's Interpretive Choices

Contextual Choices

> *Problem in the Interpreters' Life Context*: African Americans in a racist setting; racism.
> *Root Problem*: Powerlessness, helplessness, being under the power of racism.

Discrimination, exclusion, marginalization, violence, and oppression in all aspects of human existence are concrete problems engendered by racism. Walker describes racism as something that clings to people so much so that they cannot (readily) separate themselves from their own racism. The root problem for believers in the African and African American contexts described by Alice Walker is powerlessness, a lack of ability. They are "under the power of racism" as well as victims of the manifestations of racism. They are "helpless" and need to be empowered. This is the blessing that the beatitudes and the gospel bring to people: They are "helped." How? By whom? This is not spelled out. But the community of the church, or "prayer band," clearly plays a central role in communicating the vision (or, in Walker's words, the special "knowledge") of a spiritual reality that empowers believers. These contextual choices are quite apparent when one compares Walker's interpretation with those of Davies and Allison, Jordan, and Strecker.

Theological Choices

> *Role of the Text as Scripture*: Empowering Word and, secondarily, Book of the Covenant or Family Album.
> *View of Discipleship:* Struggling for God's kingdom and God's justice.
> *View of the Moral Life:* Liberationist.

Believers (disciples) are people who live according to a special vision of spiritual reality (the kingdom) and struggle for peace and harmony among human beings in their "differentness." They seek harmony with the universe in its diversity. They struggle "for God's kingdom and God's justice" (Matt. 6:33). These are their primary characteristics.

When one compares Alice Walker's view of the moral life with those of Davies and Allison, Jordan, and Strecker, it appears that, unlike them, Walker presupposes a "liberationist" view of the moral life. According to this view, in order to have a good moral life, one needs to be freed (liberated) from oppressive powers (here, racism) and to contribute to freeing others from it.

Scripture and its authoritative interpretation—"The Gospel According to Shug"—function primarily as an "empowering word" and also as a "book of the covenant or family album": They empower by allowing believers to recognize themselves as part of God's people or family, the family of the Creator and of the Mother.

Textual Choices

> *Most Significant Textual Features:* **"in front of the text"**; the descriptions of oppressed and marginalized people (the poor in spirit, those who mourn, those who are meek because they are crushed by oppression, those who are hungry for justice) and the promise of reversal of injustice (theirs is the kingdom, they will be comforted, they will inherit the land, they will be filled)
> *Methods:* Voices from the margin.

Although Alice Walker does not make her analysis of Matthew 5:3-12 (and other parts of the Sermon on the Mount) explicit, her interpretation rests on the textual dimensions we call "in front of the text"; we can even suggest that she used a method akin to the "voices from the margin" critical method. This is apparent as we contrast Walker's interpretation with those of Davies and Allison, Jordan, and Strecker. For instance, she identifies the "poor in spirit," not as people with a proper humble attitude (as Strecker does), but as marginalized people who are "crushed in spirit," depressed because they are under the power of racism, victims of its manifestations, and marginalized as "illegitimate." Conversely, the promises are understood as reversals of situations of injustice. The basis for this interpretation is the translation of the Greek *dikaiosune* (5:6, 10) as "justice," rather than "righteousness." This is further strengthened by the translation of *gê* (5:5) as "inherit the land" (from which the poor have been deprived) or "inherit the creation" (emphasized by Walker).[35]

3. Clarence Jordan, *The Cotton Patch Version of Matthew and John* and *The Sermon on the Mount*[36]

The Teaching of the Beatitudes for Believers According to Jordan

Clarence Jordan interpreted the Sermon on the Mount and its teaching about the kingdom of God on earth not only through his writing, but also through the foundation, in 1942, of the Koinonia Farm in Americus, Georgia. This pioneering interracial farming community in the heart of the American Deep South made significant contribution to the development of scientific farming in the area, even as its witness against racial prejudice made it the object of hostility. "The purpose of the 'cotton patch' approach to the scriptures," says Jordan, "is to help the modern reader to have the same sense of participation in them which the early Christians must have had."[37] The point is to produce not a technically correct translation, but a translation that conveys the effect of a passage. For instance, after pointing out that we have "emptied the term 'crucifixion' of its original content of terrific emotion, of violence, of indignity and stigma, of defeat," Jordan says, "I have translated it as 'lynching,' well aware that this is not technically correct."[38]

Here are the three first beatitudes in the "cotton patch version":

> The spiritually humble are God's people, for they are citizens of his new order.
> They who are deeply concerned are God's people, for they will see their ideas become reality.
> They who are gentle are his people, for they will be his partners across the land.[39]

For Jordan, the beatitudes are a stairway to spiritual life. They are steps into the kingdom; or we might call them stages in the naturalization of the kingdom citizen. First, in forsaking one s old country the world the spiritual immigrant must feel a deep dissatisfaction with the old citizenship and sense a real need for the new. Second, recognizing that citizenship is a gift that can never be obtained on one's own, the spiritual immigrant knows that it is crucial to be concerned enough to leave the old and make the journey to the new land. Third, when the immigrant gets to the new land, he or she must renounce all former allegiances and make a commitment of complete loyalty to the will and way of the adopted country. In the words of the Sermon on the Mount, the kingdom citizen must be "poor in spirit," then a "mourner," and then "meek."[40]

Each of the other beatitudes is another "step into the kingdom." The next one, "They who have an unsatisfied appetite for the right are God's people, for they will be given plenty to chew on,"[41] expresses Jesus' claim "that kingdom citizens who had really submitted themselves to God would have a deep and genuine desire for the righteousness of the kingdom, instead of a mock hunger for that which has been falsely branded 'righteousness.'"[42] Consequently, in the next steps of the "stairway to spiritual life," those who are God's people are "merciful" in that they are "those who have an attitude of such compassion toward all people that they want to share gladly all that they have with one another and with the world."[43] Then, as "the pure in heart" who are "partakers of the divine blessing," "[t]hose whose motives are pure,"[44] "shall see God now;

it is not a matter of waiting until we get to heaven. . . . But they not only shall see God, they shall be like God. 'The peacemakers are partakers of the divine blessing, for they shall be called children of God.' . . . God the Father is a peacemaker. Quite naturally, little peacemakers, bearing his image, 'shall be called children of God.' . . . God's plan of making peace is not merely to bring about an outward settlement between evil people but to create people of goodwill."[45]

Jordan's Interpretive Choices

Contextual Choices

> *Problem in the Interpreters' Life Context:* Prejudice and racism in the American Deep South.
> *Root Problem:* Lack of will to immigrate to God's kingdom.

The root problem is that the readers of the beatitudes lack the will to begin spiritual immigration. Jordan's interpretation presupposes that the goal of the beatitudes is to entice the readers to begin this immigration. The solution to this problem is the creation of "people of goodwill." In contrast to Walker's interpretation, it is clear that for Jordan the contextual problem—prejudice and racism in the Deep South—is primarily the result of bad will. Segregationists and racists need to be convinced of the goodness of abandoning all former allegiances to the world in order to embrace life in the kingdom.

Theological Choices

> *Role of the Text as Scripture:* Stairway to Spiritual Life.
> *View of Discipleship:* An ongoing process of "spiritual immigration," becoming kingdom citizens.
> *View of the Moral Life:* Consequentialist.

A stairway to spiritual life, steps into the kingdom, becoming kingdom citizen, making the journey to the new land, being spiritual immigrants, these are Jordan's primary theological concepts. Discipleship is conceived as an ongoing process, a journey in which the beatitudes invite us to participate.

When we compare the views of the moral life of Davies and Allison (perfectionist), Walker (liberationist), and Strecker (deontological), with that of Jordan, it appears that, unlike them, Jordan presupposes that the "good" is assessed in terms of the ultimate outcome (here, becoming a kingdom citizen), the ultimate "consequences" of one's action. Jordan's view of the moral life is, therefore, best described as consequentialist, a view according to which one can properly envision and have a good moral life when decisions are made on the basis of an assessment of the potential outcome of the envisioned action.

When we compare the role of Scripture in Jordan's interpretation with the list of metaphors on pages 27-28, it becomes clear that Jordan has proposed his own metaphor for the role of the beatitudes as Scripture, "stairway to spiritual life." This metaphor combines features of Scripture as a "lamp to my feet," giving a sense of direction to spiritual life, and as "good news" offering access to spiritual realm.[46]

Textual Choices

Most Significant Textual Features: **"within the text"**; the progression from one beatitude to the other and how this progression relates to becoming a disciple (an immigrant in the kingdom).
Methods: Narrative criticism (implicitly).

Jordan does not define his analytical method for identifying the most significant features of the beatitudes. However, since the goal is to help the modern reader have a "sense of participation" in the text, Jordan's approach implicitly emphasizes the narrative textual dimension. Because the unfolding of the plot and the roles of the characters in it are highlighted as the most significant aspects of the text, readers can readily identify with one character or another. In this case, the beatitudes are near the beginning (Matt. 4:18) of the story about Jesus making disciples, in which the readers are invited to participate, as Jordan explicitly notes.[47]

4. Georg Strecker, The Sermon on the Mount

The Teaching of the Beatitudes for Believers According to Strecker[48]

Georg Strecker writes regarding Matthew 5:3: "As entrance requirement for the kingdom of God, the first beatitude formulates an indirect demand. Admittance to the *eschaton* [the end of time (and its kingdom)] is linked to the requirement [to be] poor in spirit."[49] The same applies to each of the beatitudes in Matthew 5:3-12. Each is an "ethical admonition" to adopt a specific behavior: to be poor in spirit, to mourn, and to be meek (three forms of humble attitude); to be hungry and thirsty for righteousness (strive to have a righteous behavior);[50] to be merciful and to be pure in heart (have a good conscience, having fulfilled the demand of righteousness);[51] to be a peacemaker; not to give up on the standard of righteousness even when persecuted for it.[52]

For Strecker, the beatitudes in Matthew are "ethical admonitions" as compared with the beatitudes in Luke 6:20-21: "Blessed are you who are poor," "Blessed are you who are hungry now," "Blessed are you who weep now." Luke's beatitudes refer to the concrete condition of the "blessed ones," actual poverty, sorrow, and hunger. By adding "in spirit" to "poor" and "for righteousness" to "hunger," Matthew has transformed these beatitudes into a call for specific moral behavior. The second part of each of the beatitudes—"yours is the kingdom of heaven," "you shall be comforted," and so on—confirms for Strecker that they are "entrance requirements for the kingdom." They are "eschatological demands," that is, demands for life in the end time.[53] Since Jesus, the Son of God, their "teacher of righteousness,"[54] is the "eschatological Lord," who reveals God's will and demands a new social behavior from his followers,[55] that end time is now. The present time is for these disciples viewed in terms of the "end."[56]

Strecker's Interpretive Choices

Contextual Choices

> *Problem in the Interpreters' Life Context:* Western culture in a nuclear age.
> *Root Problem:* Lack of knowledge of the basic moral principles of God's will.

Strecker, a biblical scholar, does not make explicit the context of his interpretation until the concluding pages of his work. Yet, throughout, he presupposes that the root problem is that the readers lack knowledge of the basic moral principles that God wants the disciples to follow. For Strecker, the beatitudes and the rest of the Sermon on the Mount are in tension with the individualistic and self-centered modes of life.[57] In this way, Strecker locates himself in Western culture. He further specifies this context when he points out that it is urgent for people to hear this teaching in a world characterized by anxiety regarding the nuclear age: "For the first time in its history, the human race sees itself not just theoretically, but actually faced with the possibility that human life on this earth could be annihilated . . . through a self-initiated atomic blast of annihilation."[58]

Textual Choices

> *Most Significant Textual Features:* **"behind the text,"** as window;
> Matthew's intention.
> *Methods:* Redaction criticism, as a historical method.

The most significant features of the text, for Strecker, are the additions ("redaction") that Matthew made to the traditions he received in this case, the beatitudes that were part of the source Q, sayings also used in Luke 6:20-23. These additions are the windows through which one can discern Matthew's intention. "The results of more than two hundred years of historical-critical research" require these conclusions.[59] These historical reconstructions have established that the Sermon on the Mount "is not a speech made by Jesus but the literary work of the Evangelist Matthew, for between the historical Jesus and the composition of the New Testament Gospels there is a broad domain of oral and written tradition within the early Christian communities."[60] Each of the Gospels, including Matthew, presents Jesus' ministry and teaching in such a way as to address the needs of Christian communities in its time and place. Why did Matthew write a Gospel "characterized by five composed speeches, the first of which is the Sermon on the Mount"? Matthew "had in mind," says Strecker, "the worship and catechetical instruction of a community that had to orient itself anew in a situation of expanding time and an expanding church . . . perhaps in the next to the last decade of the first century in a Greek-speaking community, presumably in Syria."[61] For this purpose, Matthew integrated the sayings of Jesus found in the source Q (sayings also used by Luke) as well as other traditions into his other source, Mark. But this is not a "scissors and paste" exercise. Matthew is a "redactor" and theologian, who also rewrites his source to emphasize what his community particularly needs. The historical-critical approach used by Strecker is called redaction criticism. The beatitudes in Matthew 5:3-12 are the result of Matthew's "redaction" (editing or rewriting) of the beatitudes found in source Q, as presented in Luke 6:20-23:

> Blessed are you who are poor, for yours is the kingdom of God.
> Blessed are you who are hungry now, for you will be filled. Blessed
> are you who weep now, for you will laugh. Blessed are you when
> people hate you, and when they exclude you, revile you, and
> defame you on account of the Son of Man. Rejoice in that day and
> leap for joy, for surely your reward is great in heaven; for that is
> what their ancestors did to the prophets.

Theological Choices

> *Role of the Text as Scripture:* Canon.
> *View of Discipleship:* "Doing God's will" as an "entrance requirement for the kingdom."
> *View of the Moral Life:* Deontological.

The theological choices of Strecker appear quite clearly when his interpretation is compared with those of Davies and Allison, Walker, and Jordan. For Strecker, the teaching of the beatitudes is constructed around three theological concepts: (1) "ethical exhortations"; (2) "entrance requirement for the kingdom"; and (3) disciples as people who "do God's will" and who are members of "a community that based its faith and its order on the life and teachings of the earthly Jesus, whom it addressed and awaited as the exalted and coming Lord."[62]

Strecker's view of the moral life is clearly different from that of Davies and Allison (perfectionist), Walker (liberationist), and Jordan (consequentialist). It is a "deontological" view of the moral life (see Emmanuel Kant), a view in which good behavior comes from implementing basic moral principles in one's life. Here, these basic moral principles (God's will as taught by the eschatological Lord) are in radical tension with the common secular life. Humility—being poor in spirit, mourning, and being meek—is praised in the beatitudes as "blessed" rather than self-confidence and self-assertiveness, which are praised by Western culture. Thus, the beatitudes also function as a call to repentance, to changed life.

For Strecker, as Scripture, the beatitudes function as "Canon." They shape the believers' moral lives as an implementation of God's will, so that the church might fulfill its mission.[63] The beatitudes as an "entrance requirement for the kingdom" provide a means of recognizing who does and does not belong to the community of believers.

II—Holding a Second Roundtable on the Beatitudes

The goal of the second roundtable discussion is threefold: (1) to help each member of the group acknowledge that she or he has made theological and textual choices while formulating her or his contextual interpretation of the teaching of the beatitudes for certain believers; (2) to identify the particular theological concepts with which she or he framed the interpretation—the particular views of discipleship, the moral life, as well as the Scripture (already partially discussed)—and (3) to verify that this interpretation is legitimately grounded in a particular dimension of the text, chosen as the most significant.

The group setting of a roundtable discussion is most important at this point because, individually, each of us finds it difficult to recognize that when we read a Bible passage, we have actual textual and theological choices to make and that we are in fact making them. As we read, did we not carefully pay attention to what the text says? Regarding discipleship, did we not simply take into account that in the beatitudes Jesus addresses the disciples (as is clear from the "you" in Matthew 5:11-12)? Regarding the view of the moral life, is this not implied in the view of discipleship presented by the text? Regarding the most significant textual dimension, did we not read Matthew 5:3-12 as a whole? It is only when we are sitting at a roundtable—with other persons whom we respect as they are, with their different interpretations—that we can truly acknowledge the distinctiveness of our own interpretation and recognize that we have made choices. The face-to-face contact of the roundtable does not allow us to dismiss those whose interpretations are different from ours, as we easily do with written interpretations with which we disagree. If we happen to disagree with Alice Walker's interpretation, it is easy to dismiss her "because she is a novelist" and not a biblical scholar; or Clarence Jordan, because he is some kind of radical activist pastor; or W. D. Davies and Dale Allison, because their scholarship is too sophisticated ; or Georg Strecker, because he is emphasizing too much the difference between Matthew and Luke. Whatever may be our rationale, it is easy to put back a book on the shelf. But if our discussion group is really a roundtable, we cannot exclude anyone, in the same way that we do not want to be excluded from the conversation. We have to take seriously every different interpretation.

We already understand why other members of our Bible study group have formulated different teachings of the text for believers in diverse concrete situations. These believers have different needs in their different contexts. But we are suspicious of these contextual interpretations, including our own. Did we not overemphasize the contextual needs of the believers? Did we not "read into the text" something that is not there? Did we not inappropriately impose on the text theological or ethical concepts about which this text has nothing to say? Of course, it is always possible we misread the text and that we need to refine or correct our interpretations of it. However, it is most likely that each of our interpretations is basically legitimate—properly grounded in the text and in dialogue with the text about an appropriate theological issue—even if it needs some refinements and adjustments.

In this second roundtable discussion, each interpretation is once again presumed to be legitimate, and all efforts are made to show it is. This positive attitude toward the diversity of interpretations is necessary, so that the group may help each of its members recognize that all made actual textual and theological choices and that all formulations of the teaching of the text are actually grounded in a significant dimension of the text and in dialogue with the text about plausible theological issues.

Suggestions for a Profitable Discussion

The Bible study group should, once again, be led by one member who assumes the role of facilitator. A scribe should record the results of the discussion and prepare a report in order to facilitate the sharing of the main results. Each member of the Bible study group should have received a copy of the scribe's report for the first roundtable—a summary of the results of the first roundtable discussion. At a glance, you can see on this report how your interpretation differs from the interpretations of the teachings of the beatitudes by other members of the group, in terms of contextual choices and views of the role of Scripture.

In addition, you should come to the second roundtable discussion on the beatitudes ready to compare your interpretation with those of Davies and Allison, Walker, Jordan, and Strecker in terms of contextual, theological, and textual choices. For this, you are invited to complete the last column of the following chart, "Summary of Interpretations," that summarizes the presentation of these interpretations. In this way, from the start of the second roundtable discussion, each member of the group can see at a glance how her or his interpretation stands vis-à-vis these four interpretations. (To facilitate the work of the scribe, you may want to give her or him a copy of the chart completed with information about your interpretation.)

Although the group members' interpretations will certainly differ in some ways from those of Davies and Allison, Walker, Jordan, and Strecker, it is nevertheless similar to one of these. Thus, one possible way for the facilitator to involve everyone in the group discussion from the outset may be to begin by asking each member to identify which of the four interpretations presented above is closest to hers or his, explaining briefly why this is the case. Then the group can progress in the discussion, following questions such as the following:

—According to your interpretation, the teaching of the beatitudes helps believers address some problem or need in their lives as believers in a particular context. What kind of problem? How does it compare with the problems presupposed by the four interpretations presented above?
—Which metaphors would best express the role of Scripture in your interpretation? What view of discipleship did your interpretation

presuppose? What view of the moral life did your interpretation pre-suppose? How does it compare with the four interpretations above?
—What kind of analytical-textual choices did you make in your own inter-pretation? What were the most significant features of the beatitudes for you? What kind of questions would help you to see more clearly this feature of the beatitudes? To which critical method are these questions more closely related? How does your choice of most significant textual dimension compare with those of the four interpretations above?
—Without abandoning your interpretation, do you see ways to refine it? To clarify how it is grounded in the text? To make it more consistent? To clarify the view of discipleship and the moral life it involves?

In all this, keep in mind that the goal of this second roundtable is for members of the group to help one another discern the specific kind of interpretive choices each made. Have a great discussion!

III—Sharing Results of a Second Roundtable on the Beatitudes

Before proceeding with the preparation of a third roundtable on the beatitudes, it is essential to take stock of the results of the second one. For this, the scribe prepares a report, on the basis of the discussion and the summary each participant has provided, comparing her or his interpre-tation with those of the authors discussed above. This is essential, so members of the group can refer to this report in the subsequent round-table, and for other groups in a plenary session of a large class that has been subdivided into several groups.

The goal of this report is to make clear how the contextual, theological, and textual choices of each of the interpretations of the members of the group compare with those found in the interpretations of Davies and Allison, Walker, Jordan, and Strecker. This report may take the form of a chart similar to the one presented above, but now about the group mem-bers' interpretations.

Interpreters' Contextual Choices	W. D. Davies and Dale C. Allison Jr.	Alice Walker	Clarence Jordan	Georg Strecker	Your Interpretation
1) Problem in the Interpreter's Life Context (see chap. 2, pp. 29-32)	1) European Americans in a post-holocaust setting: concerns for the relationship between Christianity and Judaism	1) African Americans in a racist setting; racism	1) Prejudice and racism in the American Deep South	1) Western culture in a nuclear age	1)
2) Root Problem (see chap. 1, pp. 29-32)	2) Lack of faith/vision of the kingdom	2) Powerlessness, helplessness, being under the power of racism	2) Lack of will to immigrate to God's kingdom	2) Lack of knowledge of the basic moral principles of God's will	2)

Interpreters' Theological Choices	W. D. Davies and Dale C. Allison Jr.	Alice Walker	Clarence Jordan	Georg Strecker	Your Interpretation
1) Role of the Text as Scripture (see chap. 1, pp. 27-28)	1) Book of the Covenant/Family Album	1) Empowering Word and, secondarily, Book of the Covenant or Family Album	1) Stairway to Spiritual Life	1) Canon	1)
2) View of Discipleship	2) Sharing in the vision of the kingdom and imitating Jesus	2) Struggling for God's kingdom and God's justice	2) An ongoing process of "spiritual immigration": becoming kingdom citizens	2) "Doing God's will" as an "entrance requirement for the kingdom"	2)
3) View of the Moral Life	3) Perfectionist	3) Liberationist	3) Consequentialist	3) Deontological	3)

Interpreters' Textual Choices	W. D. Davies and Dale C. Allison Jr.	Alice Walker	Clarence Jordan	Georg Strecker	Your Interpretation
1) Most Significant Textual Features (see chap. 2, pp. 54-57)	1) "within the text"; figurative and symbolic message; style; allusions to the Septuagint, Jewish traditions, and other New Testament texts	1) "in front of the text"; descriptions of oppressed and marginalized people (the poor in spirit) and the promise of reversal of injustice (kingdom, comfort, and so on)	1) "within the text"; the progression from one beatitude to the other and how this progression relates to becoming a disciple (an immigrant in the kingdom)	1) "behind the text"; as window; Matthew's intention	1)
2) Methods (see chap. 2, pp. 54-57)	2) Literary criticism, with history of traditions and literary form of redaction criticism	2) Voices from the margin	2) Narrative criticism (implicitly).	2) Redaction criticism, as a historical method	2)

Notes

1. This is something biblical scholars learned from specialists in hermeneutics, who emphasized that there is no interpretation without theological presuppositions (or more generally, conceptual or hermeneutical presuppositions), and from feminists and other advocacy interpreters who underscored the very concrete contextual choices involved in the most sophisticated analytical interpretations.

2. For a detailed discussion and justification of these three interpretive frames, see "Overture: Reception, Critical Interpretations, and Scriptural Criticism," in *Reading Israel in Romans: Legitimacy and Plausibility of Different Interpretations*, ed. Cristina Grenholm and Daniel Patte (Harrisburg, Pa.: Trinity Press International, 2000), 1-54.

3. See below, the section "Holding a Second Roundtable Discussion on the Beatitudes" for more direct suggestions on how we hope you will want to make use of our presentation of these four interpretations of the Beatitudes.

4. W. D. Davies and Dale C. Allison Jr., *The Gospel According to Saint Matthew*, vol. 1, International Critical Commentary (Edinburgh: T & T Clark, 1988), 429-69, especially 466-67.

5. Ibid., 466; see also 439-40.

6. Ibid., 466.

7. Ibid.; see also 436-39.

8. Ibid., 467.

9. Ibid.

10. Ibid., 1-7.

11. Ibid., 423-27.

12. Ibid., 442-66.

13. Ibid., 427.

14. Ibid.

15. Ibid., 466.

16. Ibid., xi.

17. Ibid., 436.

18. Ibid., 437.

19. Ibid., 33.

20. Alice Walker, *The Temple of My Familiar* (San Diego: Harcourt Brace Jovanovich, 1989), 287-89. You might want to read the passage entitled "The Gospel According to Shug."

21. Ibid., 287.

22. Alice Walker, *The Color Purple: A Novel* (New York: Harcourt Brace Jovanovich, 1982).

23. Walker, *Temple of My Familiar*, 299.

24. Ibid., 300.

25. Ibid., 304.

26. Ibid., 302.

27. Ibid., 294.

28. Ibid., 289.

29. Ibid., 294-95.

30. Ibid., 299.

31. As is suggested in ibid., 295.

32. Ibid., 289.

33. Ibid., 287-89.

34. Ibid.

35. This latter type of interpretation is found in Warren Carter, *Matthew and the Margins: A Sociopolitical and Religious Reading* (Maryknoll, N.Y.: Orbis Books, 2000), 130-37.

36. Clarence Jordan, *The Cotton Patch Version of Matthew and John* (Clinton, N.J.: New Win Publishing, 1970) and *The Sermon on the Mount* (Valley Forge, Pa.: Judson Press, 1952).

37. Jordan, *Cotton Patch*, 9.

38. Ibid., 10.

39. Ibid., 22.

40. Jordan, *Sermon on the Mount*, 15.

41. Jordan, *Cotton Patch*, 22.

42. Jordan, *Sermon on the Mount*, 17.

43. Ibid.

44. Jordan, *Cotton Patch*, 22.

45. Jordan, *Sermon on the Mount*, 18-20.

46. A question you may want to ponder: How related is Jordan's interpretation to Augustine's interpretation, found in chapter 1?

47. Jordan, *Sermon on the Mount*, 1-6.

48. Georg Strecker, *The Sermon on the Mount: An Exegetical Commentary*, trans. O. C. Dean, Jr. (Nashville: Abingdon Press, 1988).

49. Ibid., 33.

50. Ibid., 37-38.

51. Ibid., 39.

52. Ibid., 42-45.

53. Ibid., 26.

54. Ibid., 45.

55. Ibid., 23.

56. Ibid., 26.

57. Ibid., 182-85.

58. Ibid., 181.

59. Ibid., 11.

60. Ibid.

61. Ibid., 14.

62. Ibid., 179.

63. Strecker underscores that this is not a teaching for "individuals" by themselves, and thus not a reading of Scripture as "lamp to my feet" (Ibid., 183).

CHAPTER 3

Reading the Beatitudes as Scripture When Violence Is Perpetrated Against Innocents: Matthew 5:3-12

Introduction: Why a Third Roundtable?

The need for a third roundtable, a different kind of roundtable, became clear during the previous group discussions.

During the first roundtable, we noted that other people around the table understood the teaching of the Beatitudes differently because they envisioned believers with different needs in different life contexts. Scriptural interpretations differ in part because readers of the Bible make different contextual choices.

During the second roundtable, you compared your own reading with interpretations by biblical scholars (Davies and Allison, and Strecker), by a pastor (Jordan), and by a novelist (Walker). This comparison showed that differences in interpretations also reflected two other kinds of interpretive choices. You viewed a specific aspect of the text as most significant; these were textual choices. In addition, you chose a certain view of discipleship and of the moral life and a correlated view of the role of the text as Scripture; these were theological choices, made as ways to enter in dialogue with the text. At the second roundtable, you recognized that the interpreter in each case had good reasons for her or his choices.

I—Preparing for a Third Roundtable on the Beatitudes

Much remains to be discussed. It is difficult to be satisfied with the conclusion that several interpretations are equally plausible. This is especially the case when one considers scriptural interpretations. There is a need for a better sense of closure. Believers need to know which of these interpretations is the Word of God, by which they should live in their context. Some interpretations are better than others, and the third roundtable in the process of scriptural criticism suggests ways to evaluate interpretations of the Bible as Scripture.

The preceding discussions may already have included some evaluations. Instinctively, you may have rejected one or several interpretations. Some members of the group were undoubtedly suspicious of interpretations that conflicted with theirs. Here is what we often hear in discussion groups:

> John has read into the text what he wanted to find in it. Jane's interpretation is biased; she distorts what the text says. These are bad faith interpretations; they refuse to hear the text's exhortations or its condemnation of a certain lifestyle.

These critical comments were premature at the earlier roundtables. They are often unfair and disingenuous. By these comments, participants imply that their own interpretation is firmly grounded in the text, while those of other participants are not, as if there had been no choice regarding what aspects of the text are most significant. It is unfair for one participant to fault another for making a different yet equally legitimate textual choice. The implication in such a case is that this participant knows exactly what the text says and does not exercise any discretion regarding the key theological issue addressed by this biblical passage, as if she or he had not chosen a particular subject matter among several about which Christian believers can enter in dialogue with this text. Thus, participants should not fault others for making different theological choices. Accordingly, such a charge implies that because this participant knows what the Bible passage says, the text has a teaching only for believers in her or his particular life context—as if another participant's choice of a teaching did not reflect her or his concerns for people's needs in a particular context. Again, participants should not fault one another for making different choices.

Does this mean that everything goes? No. That no interpretation is "better" than others? No. Yet assessing the relative value of biblical interpretations needs to proceed with caution and respect for other interpreters.

The first rule is that an interpretation must be grounded in the text. Each member of the study group must be ready to show that he or she has *not* read into the text something that is not there, by pointing out the specific textual features upon which the interpretation is based. Conversely, participants should be slow to claim that someone else's interpretation is not properly grounded in the biblical passage. Such accusations are often unfair and hurtful.

Yet you may remain suspicious of interpretations of the beatitudes that contradict your own, especially when yours was formulated from your own perspective as a believer. In such a case, these other interpretations may conflict with your perception of the Word of God for us. Since this is a Word we live by, which has implications in our daily life, such a conflict of interpretation becomes quite emotional. The same is true if the beatitudes are understood to reject a religious reading that you find dangerous or hurtful. The stance is no less emotional.

The third roundtable should address these emotional issues. The finger pointing against bad interpretations is most often a value judgment against the proposed "teachings for believers." These teachings threaten some of your basic convictions, or, alternatively, you feel that such teachings are hurtful for those for whom you may feel responsible. In sum, participants often reject teachings because of love for God (because of convictions) or because of love for neighbor (for whom they feel responsible).

Assessing the value of interpretations in terms of these two basic criteria—loving God and loving neighbor—is appropriate. But you need to do so openly and explicitly. This will be the goal of the third roundtable.

Clearing the Table for the Third Roundtable

In order to proceed with this third roundtable, the first task is to clear up any misleading issues. In particular, you should acknowledge that most of the interpretations you reject are actually grounded on the text, despite the impression that participants may be reading into the text something that is not there. It is simply true that when you focus attention on certain significant features of the text (as one must to make sense of the text), that interpreter becomes blind to other aspects of the text. This point has already been made but may be clarified once again with an example.

If the rewards for being persecuted are taken as most significant, these verses (Matt. 5:10-12) become the key to the rest of the beatitudes. The beatitudes become exhortations to certain kinds of behavior. The beatitudes exhort Christian believers to become poor in spirit, to mourn, to be meek, to thirst for righteousness, to be merciful, to be pure in heart, and to be peacemakers. The end of each beatitude—theirs is the kingdom, they will be comforted, and so on—is a promised reward for righteous behavior. This is a very plausible reading. In fact, it is Strecker's reading. By adopting this perspective, Strecker is blind to other dimensions of the text. For instance, it is impossible to see allusions to depressed, oppressed, and marginalized people. These people become invisible. Yet they are there in the text. In order to see them, one must view the relation between the descriptions of the blessed ones and the promises, especially in the first four beatitudes (Matt. 5:3-6) as most significant. The poor in spirit are people who need to receive the kingdom of heaven; those who mourn need to be comforted; the meek (who did not resist when their possessions were taken away from them, including their inherited land) need to inherit the land; those who hunger and thirst for justice (because they suffer injustice) need to be filled, that is, to be treated with justice. In this interpretation, the merciful, the pure in heart, the peacemakers, and those who are persecuted for justice are those who identify themselves with the oppressed and strive for the kingdom and God's justice, as Matthew 6:33 is then translated. This is Alice Walker's interpretation.

It is appropriate to ask each interpreter to explain how her or his interpretation is grounded in the text. This is what was done during the second roundtable. Now, in this third roundtable, we can assume that all of the interpretations remaining around the table are appropriately grounded on one or another aspect of the text. Now we are ready to debate. Which of these interpretations is best?

The Third Roundtable as Quest for Consensus

This third discussion is still a roundtable. As previously, you should respect one another's opinions. Yet now the discussion takes the form of a debate because its ultimate goal is to arrive at a consensus.

Each participant comes to this roundtable with a clear idea regarding the best interpretation. Yet members of the group will not agree about their respective choices of the "best" interpretation. The previous roundtables have shown that all these choices are plausible. Yet this disagreement should not remain, as if it does not matter what interpretations others have chosen; as if we could say, I have my interpretation, and you have yours, and it does not matter that they are not the same. Biblical interpretations always matter. Christians live by their interpretations, and through their lifestyle and their actions they affect others. So these choices directly or indirectly affect everyone around them. The choice of an interpretation as the best is not a private matter. It is of interest to each person in the group, including any who do not identify themselves as Christians, because each of us is affected by Christians, who live according to their understanding of the Bible as Scripture.

You should strive toward a consensus regarding "the best" interpretation. Such a consensus is not easy to reach. Indeed, it may prove to be impossible. A more modest goal would be to achieve a consensus regarding "the worst" biblical interpretations. Even this may prove challenging.

This kind of debate is necessary because of the sordid history of biblical interpretation. There are remarkable and awe-inspiring biblical interpretations, through which the lives of many people have been transformed for the better. There are also biblical interpretations that are less than inspiring. Such interpretations of the Bible have, in the past, condoned or fueled slavery; segregation and apartheid (until recently, in South Africa); anti-Semitism, and ultimately the Jewish Holocaust or Shoah; the abuse of women; and the colonization and exploitation of other people. These (and many other) interpretations of the Bible were a transgression of God's will and a dishonoring of God, as well as crimes against neighbors. Even if you cannot reach a consensus regarding which interpretation of the Beatitudes is the best, you should at least strive to reach a consensus regarding which interpretations are most dangerous.

Even this more modest goal will not be easy to reach. So debate! Put on the table the positive and the negative aspects of each interpretation, and debate the pro and con of each interpretation.

Before starting this debate, you should be clear that your disagreements concern religious, and therefore emotional, issues. For each participant, it is self-evident that one or another interpretation is the best or the worst. It is a matter of conviction, of self-evident truth, and thus of faith. It is also a matter of gut feelings, of good or bad conscience, of elation in the presence of something delightful and beautiful, or of horror when confronted by unspeakable suffering and evil.

You should therefore be mindful that you are dealing with sensitive issues for everyone, whether Christians or bystanders observing from the outside what the natives are doing. Respect for one another's views is called for. Respecting one another also involves telling one another how we affect one another, especially when someone hurts members of the group or their neighbors.

Ground Rules for Discussion and Debate

In the first roundtable, it was most helpful for each member of the group to formulate the teaching of the Beatitudes for believers in a concrete situation. The diversity of these situations helped you see broad differences in your interpretations. These differences appear much more sharply when the discussion is focused on a single, concrete life context to which all the members of the group can relate. From this perspective, it becomes clear that the choice of one interpretation rather than another matters. The choice directly affects believers and other people in their context.

The following is a general suggestion that you will want to make more specific for your group. Some ground rules for preparing for and conducting this third roundtable are also provided.

A Concrete Life Context for the Debate

We propose to focus this debate on situations in which believers are in the presence of manifestations of violence perpetrated against innocent people. Select such a situation. Be specific.

An appropriate instance would be the terrorist attacks of September 11, 2001, against the World Trade Center in New York City and the Pentagon in Washington, D.C. with airplanes filled with passengers. There are unfortunately many other cases of violence against innocent people.

Regarding this kind of life context, appropriate questions include: How does each given interpretation of the beatitudes

- address the personal needs of Christians? (What are these needs?)
- help them address the needs of the victims? (What are these needs? What kind of help do believers need in order to minister to the victims?)
- help them have an appropriate *Christian* attitude toward the perpetrators of violence? (Who are they? Why are they violent? What do they need from believers? How can their violence be stopped or prevented?)
- help believers as disciples address the needs of the larger community threatened by this violence? (What is the nature of this threat? How should Christians address a sense of vulnerability?)
- What are the attitudes, responses, and actions by believers as disciples that will bring glory to God (such that people seeing their good works may "give glory to your Father in heaven" [Matt. 5:16])?

II—Holding a Third Roundtable on the Beatitudes

Since this debate will involve potentially emotional issues, it is better that the debate not be directly focused on the relative values of the personal interpretations of the members of the group, though you should assess the value of your own interpretation individually. The debate should be focused on the relative values of the four interpretations presented in chapter 2: Davies and Allison's, Walker's, Jordan's, and Strecker's.

This debate should be led by four individuals, each arguing in favor of one of the four interpretations: Why interpretation A is better than interpretations X, Y, and Z; and conversely, why the latter are worse than the former.

Better or worse in what sense? Exclusively in terms of these two criteria: loving God and loving neighbors. The textual issues (whether or not each is appropriately grounded in the text) and the theological issues (whether or not each presupposes appropriate views of discipleship, the moral life, and Scripture) are not to be debated. Regarding these four interpretations, these issues have been addressed already in the preceding chapter and the second roundtable. All of them have been shown to be legitimately grounded in the text and have made plausible theological choices. The two questions that each debater needs to address from his or her point of view are: Which is the best or the worst in terms of the basic Christian convictions of each of the debaters? In terms of the ways in which each interpretation affects the victims of violence, the perpetrators of violence, and the bystanders?[1]

In sum: Choose a specific life context in which believers are in the presence of manifestations of violence perpetrated against innocent people; choose leaders who will open the debate; and make sure to leave time for the rest of the group to participate in the discussion! If everyone has prepared for this debate, there will be a lively discussion. Simply keep in mind that the goal is consensus. Listen to and respect one another.

The role of facilitator is, as always, to make sure each member of the group can be heard. Yet she or he has also the responsibility to lead the group toward a consensus. Following the formal debate, a poll may be taken to discern the majority and minority opinions regarding the best and the worse interpretations in the chosen context. Following the debate, the facilitator should make sure the minority arguments are heard. Progress toward a consensus requires the participants to hear from both sides what the objections are to the other choice of best and worse interpretations and what it would take to change their minds. A way toward consensus is often to emphasize the specificity of the circumstances in the chosen life context and the different assessments of the problems and needs in these circumstances from the perspective of each of the four interpretations of the Beatitudes.

III—Sharing Results of a Third Roundtable on the Beatitudes

As usual, a scribe prepares a report on the discussion to be shared with the members of the group and in a plenary session of all the groups of a larger class. This report should briefly present the majority and minority opinions and the move toward consensus. Yet it should take the form of a collective statement from the group, presenting the points of agreement among the members including the points about which the participants have agreed to disagree.

Note

1. The moderator of the debate—usually the instructor or leader of the Bible study group—might want to intervene to make sure that each of the four interpretations is discussed.

CHAPTER 4

Jesus and the Canaanite Woman: Matthew 15:21-28

Introduction: Preparing for the Roundtables on Matthew 15:21-28

For this second key passage in the Gospel according to Matthew, you will follow a procedure that should by now be familiar:[1]

1. You should: (a) prepare for a first roundtable by formulating a contextual interpretation of Matthew 15:21-28 and comparing its contextual choices with those of a meditation on this text by the Rev. Robert Wisnewski (see below); (b) hold the first roundtable on this passage, emphasizing the differences between their respective *contextual choices*; and (c) compile and share the results of the discussion among members of the group and with other groups.

2. You should prepare for, hold, and share the results of a second roundtable by entering into dialogue with authors who published their interpretations of Matthew 15:21-28: Robert C. Wisnewski Jr., a preacher; Warren Carter and Leticia Guardiola-Saenz, two biblical scholars; Jean Colombe, a painter; and Amy-Jill Levine, another biblical scholar. In this way, you will clarify their contextual, theological,

and textual choices by comparing them with those of these five interpreters.

3. You should prepare for, hold, and share the results of a third round-table on Matthew 15:21-38 regarding the relative value of the teaching of the text for believers in the interpretations of the five authors discussed in the second roundtable. This will involve considering how these diverse teachings apply in a particular situation today.

I—First Roundtable on Matthew 15:21-28

A) Preparing the First Roundtable

Following is the text of Matthew 15:21-38, in the NRSV translation, with some alternate translations that reflect the published interpretations we will discuss:

> Matthew 15:21—Jesus left that place and went away to the district of Tyre and Sidon.
> 22—Just then a Canaanite woman from that region came out and started shouting [crying out], "Have mercy on me, Lord [Master], Son of David; my daughter is tormented by a demon."
> 23—But he did not answer her at all. And his disciples came and urged him, saying, "Send her away, for she keeps shouting [crying out] after us."
> 24—He answered, "I was sent only to the lost sheep of the house of Israel."
> 25—But she came and knelt before him, saying, "Lord [Master], help me."
> 26—He answered, "It is not fair to take the children's food and throw it to the dogs [puppies]."
> 27—She said, "Yes, Lord [Master], yet even the dogs [puppies] eat the crumbs that fall from their masters' [lords'] table."
> 28—Then Jesus answered her, "Woman, great is your faith! Let it be done for you as you wish." And her daughter was healed instantly.

You should now prepare for the first roundtable discussion on Matthew 15:21-28. For this, you should:

1) Formulate in writing a contextual interpretation of this Bible passage presenting the teaching of Matthew 15:21-28 for believers in a specific life context of their choice. See chapter 1. Use the form printed on pages 29-32.

2) Compare your interpretation and your contextual choices with the

Reverend Wisnewski's meditation on this passage. This exercise will help you better recognize the uniqueness of your own choices. Here is an excerpt from the Reverend Wisnewski's meditation on the Canaanite woman.[2]

The Teaching of Matthew 15:21-28 for Believers According to Wisnewski: "Daddy, Don't Be Ridiculous!"

I was serving ice cream one night after supper some years ago when the kids were younger. As I scooped out the servings, Meg looked at her bowl and Rob's and saw an injustice being done. "Why did you give Rob more than me?" she asked. "Because I love Rob more than I love you," I replied. Meg looked at me and said, "Daddy, don't be ridiculous." My words, saying one thing, actually emphasized something altogether different. The words of Jesus in the passage will emphasize something different as well. He also may be using the term to help teach the woman something as well. Has she bought into the oppression in which she is held? Does she believe she is less than others? Jesus may be feeling her out a bit as well. It's interesting to me that the word Jesus uses for dog is the diminutive term, more like puppy or pet dog. When I told Meg I loved Rob more there was a tone in my voice that helped her know the words weren't true. The same thing is going on here with the Canaanite woman. Jesus uses the term but with a tone that helps her see that she isn't a dog. The woman seems further drawn in by Jesus' tone here and says that even dogs get crumbs from the table that the children don't want. She's not asking for the whole feast here, just a little of what is left over.

Teaching of the Text for Whom?	Rev. Wisnewski's Interpretation	Your Interpretation of Matthew 15:21-38
1) For what kind of believers?	1) The text challenges contemporary Canaanite women with the news that Jesus' hurtful words actually mean something altogether different when believers focus on how it is said, instead of what is said.	1)
2) What specific personal, social, cultural, and religious context is presupposed by this teaching? In other words, what aspects of believers' lives are being addressed?	2) Based on that anecdote about his children and ice cream, Wisnewski tries to address believers' experiences of injustice (as is explained in the rest of the meditation). He tries to relate to believers who are modern-day Canaanite women, who are treated like dogs and end up buying into the oppression in which [they are] held and believe [they are] less than others.	2)
3) What specific needs or problems in this context are being addressed? A lack of knowledge (what kind?), a lack of ability (to do what?), a lack of faith or vision (what kind?), a lack of will (to effect what?)?	3) Wisnewski, we think, is trying to challenge the lack of faith or vision by modern-day Canaanite women who buy into their oppression and see themselves as their oppressors and their accomplices see them, instead of seeing themselves as Jesus sees them as a loving father sees his children.	3)
4) How does this teaching address, challenge, and transform these problems or needs? What metaphor would best represent this function?	4) The text as family album helps believers see themselves as loved children of God, rather than as worthless outsiders.	4)

B) First Roundtable Discussion on Matthew 15:21-28

Hold the first roundtable discussion under the leadership of a member facilitator, noting the differences among the group's interpretations regarding your respective choices: in contexts; in aspects of life in this context for which believers have needs; in root problems (lack of knowledge, of ability, and so on); in teachings through which this Bible passage addresses these needs and root problems; and in the roles of Scripture they presupposed.

C) Sharing Results

Under the leadership of a member scribe, compile and share the results of the first roundtable in preparation for the second roundtable.

II—Second Roundtable on Matthew 15:21-28

A) Preparing the Second Roundtable Discussion

In order to clarify your own contextual, theological, and textual choices, you should compare them with those of other interpreters who have published their interpretations. We first review Wisnewski's interpretive choices. Then, we present an analysis of the interpretive choices made by Warner Carter and Leticia Guardiola-Saenz, two biblical scholars, in their respective interpretations of Matthew 15:21-28. Then we invite the participants to identify by themselves the interpretive choices found in two interpretations of this Bible passage (Matt. 15:21-28): an artistic interpretation in a painting by Jean Colombe and a scholarly interpretation by Amy-Jill Levine.

1) Robert C. Wisnewski Jr.'s Interpretive Choices

Contextual Choices

> *Problem in the Interpreters' Life Context*: Experiences of injustice, oppression, being made to feel worthless.
> *Root Problem*: Lack of faith or vision that one is a part of God's family.

Theological Choices

> *Role of the Text as Scripture*: Family Album.
> *Theological Concepts*: Jesus as a loving father.

The primary theological concept in the Reverend Wisnewski's meditation is Jesus as loving father. Wisnewski presents a Jesus who does not humiliate the woman, but instead, like a father talking with his child, challenges her to claim what she needs.

Textual Choices

> *Most Significant Textual Features*: **"behind the text"**; the historical reality to which the text as window refers.
> *Methods*: Historical criticism (and philology, that is, study of the Greek vocabulary).

Wisnewski's reading builds on the traditional historical information about Canaanites and about the ambiguity of the textual vocabulary—though not explicitly. This is appropriate for a meditation. He takes into account that Jesus and the Canaanite woman meet in the territory of Tyre and Sidon, a place where ethnic and religious tension and prejudice were strong.[3] In addition, Wisnewski underscores the nuances of the Greek, noting that the Greek word for dogs can also be translated puppies.

2) Warren Carter on Matthew 15:21-28: Recognizing Israel's Temporal Priority[4]

The Teaching of Matthew 15:21-28 for Believers According to Carter

Carter argues that this scene continues the emerging Matthean theme that ethnicity does not constitute God's people and that believing Gentiles are included in God's purposes.[5] The scene recognizes Israel's temporal priority in God's purposes as God's chosen people, but this understanding does not mean that Gentiles are excluded. Jesus, a Jew, is the agent of God's blessing for the Gentile woman. The scene locates Jesus in a world of ethnic, cultural, economic, political, and religious barriers. Jesus is not exempt from these prejudices, but God's reign, responsible for wholeness and plenty, breaks them down.[6] Carter continues: The Gentile woman is geographically on the margins of Israel and is, as a Gentile, marginal in Israel's worldview. As a Canaanite, a member of a cursed people destined to be subjugated as slaves (Gen. 9:25), she belongs to a people dispossessed by Israel's occupation and possession of the land. This Israelite victory was viewed as God's gift, was understood as an expression of Israel's elect status, and was celebrated in Israel's traditions. Yet, though submissive, she challenges this exclusive ideology. Her demand for inclusion constitutes her faith, the means by which she encounters the blessing of Israel's God. Jesus commends it as great (Matt. 15:28), in contrast with Peter's and the disciples' little faith (Matt. 14:31) and its absence from the crowds and religious leaders.[7] In sum, for Carter, in performing the miracle, Jesus overcomes ethnic, cultural, political, gender, and religious barriers.[8]

Carter's Interpretive Choices

Contextual Choices

> *Problem in the Interpreters' Life Context*: Cultural, economic, political, and religious barriers for those on the margins of power.
> *Root Problem*: A lack of vision that engenders powerlessness.

Since for Carter, the text teaches that God's reign, responsible for wholeness and plenty, breaks down cultural, economic, political, and religious barriers, the passage addresses the specific social, cultural, and religious context of Matthew's time: the reality of empire. In his introduction, Carter argues that Matthew's anti-imperial rhetoric is as relevant today as it was in antiquity because the church still finds itself at the margins of power.[9] The specific root problem being addressed is lack of vision that engenders powerlessness. The Canaanite woman, like other marginalized characters in Matthew's Gospel, represents faith communities, then and now, that find themselves removed from religious and political power centers and lack the faith or vision that would allow them to recognize the presence of God's reign. The realization that they are part of God's alternative empire, that God is on their side, subverts power structures in their favor.

Theological Choices

> *Role of the Text as Scripture*: Corrective Glasses.
> *Theological Concepts*: Ethnicity; who belongs to God's people

Since through this text believers gain the realization that they are part of God's alternative empire, we can say that the interpreters use the text as corrective glasses that allow them to see the reality of their life in a new way, recognizing in it God's alternative empire, and, as a result, being empowered by this vision.

Ethnicity does not constitute God's people. This is the overarching theme of Matthew for Carter. Carter, who grew up in New Zealand, makes explicit in his book's introduction his agenda in favor of the ethnically marginalized.

Textual Choices

> *Most Significant Textual Features*: Both **"behind the text"** and **"in front of the text"**; the marginalized communities, the subaltern in antiquity and today.
>
> *Methods*: Reader-centered, sociological, economic, and political criticisms

Carter is using social-scientific methods to ground his arguments in his commentary. He presupposes that the text is window on the ancient world, but he privileges the marginalized communities, the subaltern in antiquity. Matthew's community represents God's alternative empire, composed of society's expendables. The gospel heralds a new empire that does not pledge allegiance to Rome or the emperor.

3) Leticia Guardiola-Saenz on Matthew 15:21-28: The Canaanite Woman Reinvading the Land[10]

The Teaching of Matthew 15:21-28 for Believers According to Guardiola-Saenz

As a Mexican-American, Guardiola-Saenz "read[s] the Canaanite woman's story with the rhetoric of the Other [a self-defined person who wants to be respected in her or his otherness] against the rhetoric of Matthew and its readers."[11] Although in Mark, we read that Jesus is the one crossing the borderlands of Tyre and Sidon, in Matthew's version (15:22), the Canaanite woman is the one crossing the borderlands.[12] Guardiola-Saenz holds that the woman is not a humble dog begging for crumbs. She is a dispossessed woman who has awakened from her position as oppressed and now is coming to confront the empire and demand her right to be treated as human.[13]

The good news of Jesus' miraculous deeds and the stories about inexhaustible food has reached the Canaanite woman, and she has come to request her indemnity. The hour of the dispossessed has come. "In the midst of the wasteland, the Canaanite woman defies, with her presence and her demand, Matthew's construction of the *basileia* [kingdom]."[14]

By asking Jesus to heal her daughter, the woman is asking for restitution that will not just vindicate her as Other, but also vindicate her oppressor as Other. "The presence of the woman as the resistant oppressed, who has gained consciousness of her oppression, is finally breaking the Totalitarian system. She is confronting the oppressor. He, in turn, realizes that he has overridden her rights and ignored her existence, but now he has been humanized by her presence. The Other that he has once treated as a dog is now giving him a lesson of human courage and love for life."[15]

Guardiola-Saenz's Interpretive Choices

Contextual Choices

> *Problem in the Interpreters' Life Context*: Political and economic impe-
> rialism; totalitarian ideology and patriarchy that dehumanizes
> Others into oppressed others, dogs.
> *Root Problem*: Powerlessness (under ideological oppression).

The text teaches contemporary Canaanites that the hour of the dispossessed has come. Guardiola-Saenz's people represent present-day
Canaanites vis-à-vis the United States hegemony. Now is the time to confront the empire and demand their right to be treated as humans, not as
dogs; to be present as Others to their oppressors; and, in the process, to
humanize their oppressors.

Guardiola-Saenz, like Carter, presupposes the reality of empire.
However, she also argues from her Mexican American perspective that
the rhetoric of Matthew and its readers, by underscoring the issue of chosenness, perpetuates a totalitarian ideology common among imperialistic
nations. But by rejecting, with honor and respect, the violent insult by
Jesus, the Canaanite woman breaks this rhetoric of Matthew and substi-
tutes for it the possibility of a rhetoric of the Other that is attuned to the
kingdom.[16]

The woman's struggle to reclaim her place at the table inspires and
empowers the present Mexican struggle to reinvade the land that was
once theirs. The teaching of the Bible passage effectively addresses a
powerlessness to effect change.

Theological Choices

> *Role of the Text as Scripture*: Empowering Word.
> *Theological concepts*: The Other, humanity in the kingdom, restora-
> tion, and chosenness (as problematic).

For Guardiola-Saenz, Matthew's totalitarian rhetoric is dismantled by
the very presence of the Canaanite woman; her story enables real flesh
and blood oppressed readers to protest and reclaim all from which they
have been dispossessed, as the woman does in the story. In sum,
Guardiola-Saenz's reading of this text functions as an empowering Word.

By reading the text in this way, Guardiola-Saenz underscores key theological concepts. The Other (in the text, the Canaanite woman, and beyond
the text) is someone to be respected in her or his otherness that defines her
or his humanity. According to Guardiola-Saenz's interpretation, this is as
it should be in the kingdom *(basileia)*. On the other hand, the theological

concept of chosenness or election is problematic. This theological concept is part of the imperialistic rhetoric of Matthew. It is shared by the readers inscribed in Matthew but is defied by the reinvading Canaanite woman of Matthew 15:21-28 and her demands for restoration.

Textual Choices

> *Most Significant Textual Features*: **"in front of the text"**; the story world that engages readers to identify with the woman; how the text affects readers.
> *Methods*: Cultural and postcolonial criticisms, voices from the margin.

Guardiola-Saenz employs cultural and postcolonial criticisms that emphasize how the text engages the readers through its story world. Furthermore, she privileges the subalterns (those marginalized because they are viewed as inferior) within the text (the Canaanite woman) and in front of the text (the powerless and marginalized readers who are empowered to become Canaanite women); the kingdom *(basileia)* is represented by the Canaanite woman who is respected in her otherness. This dimension of the text is distinguished from the rhetoric of Matthew's Gospel. The rhetoric within the text represents God's *basileia* (kingdom) in the image of totalitarianism and imperial expansion, and so perpetuates both.

4) Jean Colombe's Artistic Interpretation of the Canaanite Woman

The cliché is that a picture is worth a thousand words. Jean Colombe's painting entitled "The Canaanite Woman" may convey an artistic interpretation of Matthew's text more than the words of many biblical scholars, theologians, or preachers. It can be analyzed as any other interpretation, even though we have to take into account its particular artistic medium.

You should ponder this painting and seek to identify the distinctiveness of Colombe's interpretation of Matthew 15:21-28. For this, you need to identify the differences between Colombe's interpretation and your interpretation as well as those of Wisnewski, Carter, and Guardiola-Saenz. As any interpreter, in his painting, Jean Colombe has made theological, textual, and contextual choices. What are the differences with the participant's interpretive choices and with those of the three authors discussed above?

As always, a variety of answers to this question are to be expected. Your Bible study group will emphasize different aspects of Colombe's artistic interpretation, since each member will compare it with her or his particular interpretation. The answers to the following questions can be recorded in the table found on pages 103-5.

We invite each of you to ponder this painting, keeping in mind the following question as you ponder Jean Colombe's painting: Can you identify what is the teaching of Matthew 15:21-28 for Colombe?

Les Très Riches Heures du Duc de Berry, Folio 164r
(The Canaanite Woman)
by Jean Colombe

The artist presents details of the text in this double miniature representing Christ's two different attitudes. Above, Jesus turns away from the Canaanite woman who implores him despite the scorn of the apostles; in a house at the right we see a woman trying to comfort the recumbent girl who is tormented by a demon. It might have been inconceivable for Colombe to imagine the mother leaving her ill child alone, thus the companion.

The text is a quotation of Psalm 25 (Psalm 24 in the Vulgate Latin translation); it may represent the words of the woman. It begins with verse 6 ("Remember, O LORD, your tender mercies and your lovingkindnesses, for they are from of old.") and ends with verse 22 ("Redeem Israel, O God, out of all its anguishes.")

In the small reproduction of the painting above, the Canaanite kneels before Jesus, who is touched by the perseverance of her faith and makes a gesture of consent; the apostles now seem to share their master's feelings.

Colombe's Interpretive Choices

Theological Choices

What are the main theological concepts that Colombe emphasizes? Some are expressed by the way Colombe represents both the persons and their relationships and interactions. How is Jesus represented in each scene? What is the significance of the differences in representation? What is different in Colombe's choice of theological concepts? What is the message that viewers may take away? In other words, what was for Colombe the teaching of Matthew 15:21-28 for believers? On this basis, is it possible to say what was for him the role of Matthew 15:21-28 as Scripture? (See the list of metaphors in chapter 1, pp. 27-28.)

Textual Choices

What are the most important features of the text for Colombe? What features did he include? What did he leave out?

Although Colombe did not use any of the present-day methods, one can discern his general approach. In view of the representation of the persons, and especially their clothes (which period?) and houses, did Colombe focus on what is "behind the text" (the text as window upon history) or in front of the text (how the text relates to the readers in Colombe's time, the fifteenth century)?

Contextual Choices

Is it possible to guess anything about Colombe's contextual choices? Some of the observations concerning his theological and textual choices may be of help. What aspects of life (private, social, cultural, or community) was he primarily concerned with? What needs did he presuppose believers have? What root problem (lack of knowledge? ability? will? faith? or vision?) did he presuppose believers had?

In summary, how could one express in a few words what was, according to Colombe, the teaching of Matthew 15:21-28 for believers?

5) Amy-Jill Levine's Interpretation of Matthew 15:21-28 and Her Interpretive Choices[17]

As with Colombe's painting, we are asking you to identify the differences between Levine's interpretation and your interpretation, Wisnewski's, Carter's, and Guardiola-Saenz's. What different interpretive choices did Levine make, as compared with those of the participant and the interpreters already discussed? For this comparison, use the table below.

Regarding Levine's theological choices, what are the theological concepts she emphasizes? What kind of textual choices does she make (use the table in chapter 2, pp. 54-57)? As for the contextual choices she made and the role of this text as Scripture (another part of her theological choices), you may extrapolate; as is often the case with biblical scholars, Levine does not speak of the teaching for believers of this text as Scripture. However, the fact that this is part of the *Women's Bible Commentary* is a clue about the presumed context.

> The roles of parents and children are complicated in the next story, when the ethnic factor is introduced. During his ministry, Jesus limits his mission and message to the house of Israel (see 10:5b-6). Nevertheless, he does come into contact with Gentiles. The episode of the Canaanite woman recalls that of the centurion (8:5-13). These healings—the only two in the gospel explicitly concerning Gentiles and accomplished from a distance—indicate both that the Gentile supplicants are worthy of Jesus' beneficence and that the gospel will eventually be extended to all people.
>
> Unlike Mark's account (7:24-30), Matthew's does not present Jesus entering Tyre and Sidon; rather the woman leaves her native land to meet Jesus. Further, she is not identified as Syro-Phoenician (Mark 7:26) but as a Canaanite. Her presence recalls the original struggle between the Hebrews and the indigenous population of the land. By meeting Jesus both on his own turf and on his own terms, the Canaanite woman acknowledges the priority of the Jews in the divine plan of salvation.
>
> The woman's faith is portrayed in the extended dialogue with Jesus. . . . The woman in Matthew addresses Jesus as Son of David (15:22b; cf. 9:27; 20:30) and thereby recalls the reference to the monarchy in the genealogy. . . . But, Jesus ignores her, and the disciples wish her to be sent away. . . . The woman overcomes Jesus' reluctance by turning to her advantage his language about taking the children's food and throwing it to the dogs. Instead of taking offense at his identification of her with the dogs, she redirects his comment and again appeals to Jesus as Lord. The woman asserts her claim and demonstrates her faith not by protesting the insult to her ethnic group but by arguing that both Gentiles (dogs) and children (Jews) are under the same authority. Her comments are made even more profound by the lack of relational terms identifying her: like other women who approach Jesus, she is not characterized as under the authority or the protection of a husband. The reference to bread in this story recollects the women and children in the two feeding narratives as well as the woman in the parable (13:13). Again the bread serves as a positive symbol, in contrast to the leaven of the Pharisees and Sadducees. These comparisons confirm Matthew's artistry as well as emphasis on the marginal and the disempowered.

B) Holding a Second Roundtable on Matthew 15:21-28

Hold the second roundtable discussion under the leadership of a member facilitator, following the guideline provided in chapter 2. Remember that the goal of the second roundtable discussion is to help the members of the group identify their theological and textual choices, further define the particular theological concepts with which they framed their interpretations, and verify that their interpretations are legitimately grounded in a particular dimension of the text, chosen as the most significant. Thus, each of the published interpretations should always be discussed in the process of comparing their interpretive choices with yours and the other participants. Even in the cases of Colombe's painting and Levine's interpretation, which you interpreted on your own, the goal remains the same: clarifying the distinctiveness of the participants' interpretations.[18] This includes for you to recognize which of the five published interpretations is closer to your own—a good basis to refine your interpretation. Thus, you should come to the roundtable after completing the following chart.

C) Sharing Results

Under the leadership of a member scribe, compile and share the results of the second roundtable. In preparation for the third roundtable, it is particularly helpful for you to be aware that your interpretation is somewhat similar to one of the five published interpretations. This report may take the form of a chart similar to the one presented above, but now it will contain interpretations of the members of the group.

Interpreters' Contextual Choices	Robert C. Wisnewski Jr.	Warren Carter	Leticia Guardiola-Saenz	Jean Colombe	Amy-Jill Levine	Your Interpretation
1) Problem in the Interpreters' Life Context (see chap. 1, pp. 29-32)	1) experiences of injustice, oppression, being made to feel worthless	1) cultural, economic, political, and religious barriers for those on the margins of power	1) political and economic imperialism; totalitarian ideology and patriarchy that dehumanizes others into oppressed others, dogs	1)	1)	1)
2) Root Problem (see chap. 1, pp. 29-32)	2) lack of faith or vision that one is a part of God's family	2) a lack of vision that engenders powerlessness.	2) powerlessness (under ideological oppression)	2)	2)	2)

Interpreters' Theological Choices	Robert C. Wisnewski Jr.	Warren Carter	Leticia Guardiola-Saenz	Jean Colombe	Amy-Jill Levine	Your Interpretation
1) Role of the Text as Scripture (see chap. 1, pp. 27-28)	1) Family Album	1) Corrective Glasses	1) Empowering Word	1)	1)	1)
2) Theological Concepts	2) Jesus as a loving father	2) Ethnicity, who belongs to God's people	2) The Other, humanity in the kingdom, restoration, and chosenness (as problematic)	2)	2)	2)

Interpreters' Textual Choices	Robert C. Wisnewski Jr.	Warren Carter	Leticia Guardiola-Saenz	Jean Colombe	Amy-Jill Levine	Your Interpretation
1) Most significant Textual Features (see chap. 2, pp. 54-57)	1) "behind the text"; the historical reality to which the text as window refers	1) both "behind the text" and "in front of the text"; the marginalized communities, the subaltern in antiquity and today	1) "in front of the text"; the story world that engages readers to identify with the woman; how the text affects readers	1)	1)	1)
2) Methods (see chap. 2, pp. 54-57)	2) Historical criticism (and philology, that is, study of the Greek vocabulary)	2) Reader-centered, sociological, economic, and political criticisms	2) Cultural and postcolonial criticisms, voices from the margin.	2)	2)	2)

III—Third Roundtable Discussion on Matthew 15:21-28

Five different interpretations of Matthew 15:21-28 are presented above. Each one is appropriately based on a significant aspect of the Bible passage. Each one is appropriately focused on a theological concept. Which one is "the best" reading? Which one is "the worst"? In order to assess the relative values of these five different interpretations, in a debate format, participants should keep in mind that for believers, Scripture as Living Word challenges them, perplexes them, transforms them, changes their vision of reality. Thus, in this third roundtable of the scriptural criticism process of Matthew 15:21-28, "the best" and "the worst" must be assessed in terms of the twofold criteria of love of God and love of neighbor. From this perspective, each of the five participants engaged in the opening debate should make a case for one of these interpretations as best and one as worst, as illustrated in the complex life context suggested below by Kwok Pui-lan.[19]

> Yes, who is this Canaanite woman?
> She is the woman down the dirty road of Calcutta.
> She is the mother of a political prisoner in Seoul.
> She is the old garment factory worker in Hong Kong.
> She is the mother whose daughter is a prostitute in Jakarta, Taipei, or Chiang Mai.
> She is also this survivor from Hiroshima.
> The woman is the poorest among the poor, the oppressed among the oppressed,
> she is at every corner of Asia,
> and she fills the Third World.
> Kwok Pui-Lan, *Discovering the Bible in the Non-Biblical World* (New York: Orbis Books, 1995), 83

In preparation for this debate, you might want to consider the following questions:

1. Asian women compose one-fourth of the world's population. Whose reading would benefit them? Whose would not? Whose would be hurtful?

2. How does this assessment fit with each participant's convictions about God and glorifying God as an individual and as a member of a faith community? Why?

3. If our criteria are still love of God and love of neighbor, which reading would be "the best" for Asian women? The "worst"?

Notes

1. We recommend a set of three roundtable sessions for this text. The second roundtable requires more input from the participants. However, because the participants' previous experience with roundtable discussions, it is possible to hold both Roundtable # 1 and Roundtable # 2 in a single session of the Bible study group. There are two conditions: (1) that the discussion group be kept quite small (allowing for at least 8 minutes per person); and (2) that the participants be well prepared for the discussion, by doing the suggested additional exercises.

2. The Rev. Robert C. Wisnewski Jr.'s meditation on the Canaanite woman, in *St. John's Episcopal Church Lenten Meditations and Great Stories of the Bible* (St. John's Episcopal Church, Montgomery, Ala., August 1998). Our analysis of Wisnewski's contextual choices reflects a comparison with our own interpretations.

3. Warren Carter, see below, also makes this point, as he mentions that Josephus, the Jewish historian, noted that "the Tyrians are our bitterest enemies" (Con Ap 1.70), and there were clashes between the Tyrians and the Jews in the 60s (*Jewish War* 2.473) (Carter, 321).

4. Warren Carter, *Matthew and the Margins: A Sociopolitical and Religious Reading* (Maryknoll, N.Y.: Orbis Books, 2000), 320-25.

5. Ibid., 320-21.

6. Ibid., 320.

7. Ibid.

8. Ibid., 325.

9. Ibid., 36-43; see also xvii-xx.

10. Leticia Guardiola-Saenz, "Borderless Women and Borderless Texts," *Semeia* 78, 69-81.

11. Ibid., 79.

12. Ibid., 74.

13. Ibid., 79.

14. Ibid., 77.

15. Ibid., 79-80.

16. Ibid., 79. "The presence of the woman as the resistant oppressed, who has gained consciousness of her oppression."

17. Amy-Jill Levine, "Matthew" in *Women's Bible Commentary: Expanded Edition with Apocrypha*, ed. Carol Newsom and Sharon Ringe (Louisville, Ky.: Westminster John Knox Press, 1998), 346.

18. This procedure is simply to ensure that the group makes explicit what its participants would be doing if the focus were on Colombe's or Levine's interpretation. As discussed in the introduction, any interpretation—including the interpretation of an interpretation—is always done from one's own perspective; it is framed by one's contextual, theological, and textual choices.

19. The moderator of the debate—usually the instructor or leader of the Bible study group—might want to intervene to make sure that each of the five interpretations is discussed.

CHAPTER 5

The Great Commission, the Church, and Its Mission: Matthew 28:16-20

Introduction: Preparing for the Roundtables on Matthew 28:16-20

As in the preceding chapters, you should prepare for, hold, and share the results of:

1. A first roundtable by preparing a contextual interpretation of Matthew 28:16-20 and comparing it with that of David Walker in *Appeal*, so as to note differences between the respective *contextual choices*;

2. A second roundtable by entering in dialogue with authors who have published their interpretations of Matthew 28:16-20 (Daniel J. Harrington, S.J., a biblical scholar in the U.S.A.; Musa W. Dube, a biblical scholar in Botswana; Hal Freeman, a Baptist preacher in the U.S.A.; and George M. Soares-Prabhu, S.J., a biblical scholar in India) and by clarifying each participant's own contextual, theological, and textual choices by comparing them with the choices of these four; and

3. A third roundtable on Matthew 28:16-20 regarding the relative

value of the teaching of the text for believers in the interpretations of the four authors discussed in the second roundtable. This will involve considering how these diverse teachings apply in a particular situation today.[1]

I—First Roundtable on Matthew 28:16-20

Here is the text of the Great Commission taken from the NRSV, with some alternate translations that reflect the published interpretations we will discuss.

> Matthew 28:16—Now the eleven disciples went to Galilee, to the mountain to which Jesus had directed them.
> 17—When they saw him, they worshiped him [paid him homage]; but some doubted [hesitated, were confused].
> 18—And Jesus came and said to them, "All authority [power] in heaven and on earth has been given to me.
> 19—Go therefore and make disciples of all nations [Gentiles], baptizing them in the name of the Father and of the Son and of the Holy Spirit,
> 20—and teaching them to obey everything that I have commanded you. And remember, I am with you always, to the end of the age."

To prepare for the first roundtable on the Great Commission, you should:

1. Formulate in writing a contextual interpretation of this Bible passage presenting *the teaching of Matthew 28:16-20 for believers in a specific life context of his or her choice.* See chapter 1. Use the form on pages 29-32. Read Matthew 28:16-20 in its literary context in Matthew 28 (see also Matthew 10). To facilitate the discussion, participants should focus on the same topic related to Matthew 28:16-20, namely, **its teaching regarding the mission of the Church** for believers in a particular life context.

Remember that there is no learning if through reading the text the readers/believers do not discover something new regarding the text itself or regarding their lives (viewed from the perspective of the text). For believers, Scripture as Living Word challenges them, perplexes them, transforms them, changes their vision of reality.

2. Compare your interpretation and its contextual choices with David

Walker's interpretation in *Appeal*. This exercise will help you better recognize your choices.

Appeal was published privately by the author, David Walker, in 1829. Grounded in Walker's understanding of the God-human relationship, the document delivered a blazing indictment of American racism and slavery.

> How can the preachers and people of America believe the Bible? Does it teach them any distinction on account of a man's color? Hearken, Americans! to the injunctions of our Lord and Master, to his humble followers.
>
> "And Jesus came and spake unto them, saying, all power is given unto me in Heaven and in earth. Go ye, therefore, and teach all nations, baptizing them in the name of the Father, and of the Son, and of the Holy Ghost. Teaching them to observe all things whatsoever I have commanded you; and lo, I am with you always, even unto the end of the world. Amen."
>
> I declare, that the very face of these injunctions appear to be of God and not of man. They do not show the slightest degree of distinction. "Go ye therefore," (says my divine Master) "and teach all nations," (or in other words, all people) "baptizing them in the name of the Father, and of the Son, and of the Holy Ghost." Do you understand the above, Americans? We are a people, notwithstanding many of you doubt it. You have the Bible in your hands, with this very injunction. Have you been to Africa, teaching the inhabitants thereof the words of the Lord Jesus? "Baptizing them in the name of the Father, and of the Son and of the Holy Ghost." Have you not, on the contrary, entered among us, and learnt us the art of throat-cutting, by setting us to fight, one against another, to take each other as prisoners of war, and sell to you for small bits of calicoes, old swords, knives, &c. to make slaves for you and your children? This being done, have you not brought us among you, in chains and hand-cuffs, like brutes, and treated us with all the cruelties and rigor your ingenuity could invent, consistent with the laws of your country . . . ? Can the American preachers appeal unto God, the Maker and Searcher of hearts, and tell him, with the Bible in their hands, that they make no distinction on account of men's color? Can they say, O God! thou knowest all things—thou knowest that we make no distinction between thy creatures, to whom we have to preach thy Word? Let them answer the Lord; and if they cannot do it in the affirmative, have they not departed from the Lord Jesus Christ, their master? But some may say, that they never had, or were in possession of religion, which made no distinction, and of course they could not have departed from it. I ask you then, in the name of the Lord, of what kind can your religion be? Can it be that which was preached by our Lord Jesus Christ from Heaven? I believe you cannot be so wicked as to tell him that his Gospel was that of *distinction*. . . . Did not God make us all as it seemed best to himself? What right, then, has one of us, to despise another, and to treat him cruel, on account of his color, which none, but the God who made it can alter?[2]

You should ask how your contextual choices compare with those of David Walker's in *Appeal*. Do you agree with the analysis of David Walker's interpretation below?[3] What is different in your interpretation? (We have left space for you to write contextual characteristics of your interpretation.)

We expect the first and the second roundtable discussions will be held together at the same session. If not, you should follow the procedures for holding and sharing the results of the first roundtable in chapter 1 and in chapter 4.

II—Second Roundtable on Matthew 28:16-20

A) Preparing the Second Roundtable Discussion

In order to clarify your contextual, theological, and textual choices, compare them with those of Harrington, Dube, Freeman, and Soares-Prabhu.

1) Daniel J. Harrington, S.J., on the Great Commission[4]

The Teaching of Matthew 28:16-20 for Believers According to Harrington

The most significant feature of the Gospel of Matthew is its Jewish dimension, according to Harrington. He develops this feature on three levels: (a) by informing readers about the Hebrew Bible and other Jewish texts that seem to have influenced Matthew's Gospel (or otherwise relate to it); (b) by highlighting the conflict among the Jews after the destruction of the Jerusalem temple in 70 A.D., and the continuation of Judaism and its nature; and (c) by ending each section with theological comments appropriate to the new relationship that exists between Jews and Christians since the Second Vatican Council.[5]

For Harrington, Matthew 28:16-20 is a summary of the entire Gospel. The passage brings out the Gospel's most important themes: The Father has given Jesus supreme and universal authority. The disciples are to share their discipleship not only with their fellow Jews, but also with non-Jews. "The spirit of the risen Jesus will guide and protect the church until God's kingdom comes in its fullness."[6] According to Harrington, these themes reflect two points especially important for Matthew's community: Theologically, as the authoritative risen Lord, Jesus is worthy of universal worship; and historically, the church and the synagogue in Matthew's area are on the way to definitive separation.[7] Therefore, Harrington concludes that the Great Commission moves the Christian

Questions for the Analysis of the Teaching of Matthew 28	Contextual Choices of David Walker's *Appeal*	Contextual Choices of Your Interpretation of the Great Commission
What aspect(s) of the believers' lives in a specific context is of primary concern?	The believers Walker envisions are primarily concerned with their lives in society and culture. *Appeal* rebukes nineteenth-century American society and Christian believers for their support of the institution of chattel slavery.	
What is the basic need or root problem addressed?	For Walker, it is a lack of *will*. He maintains that American preachers (European American society in general) lack the will to engage African enslaved people with the equality and respect demanded by God.	
How does this teaching address the need or root problem? What is the role of Scripture?	Walker presents the Bible as the great equalizer. The Bible equalizes the status of human beings in the sight of God. Therefore, the Bible as scripture presents a view of appropriate (holy) human relationships as those governed by the love of God that makes no distinction.	

missionary movement away from its focus on the Jewish community toward an emphasis on the Gentile community.

Harrington's Interpretive Choices

Contextual Choices

> *Problem in the Interpreters' Life Context*: the believers' lives in relationship with people of different religious convictions
> *Root Problem*: a lack of knowledge of God's will and powerlessness

In this scholarly interpretation, the teaching for believers is not made explicit. Yet one can discern that (1) the aspect of the Christians' lives that is of primary concern is their relationship with people of different religious convictions; and that (2) the basic need or root problem is a lack of knowledge regarding God's will and a feeling of powerlessness. Harrington emphasizes the disciples' appropriate response—worship—when seeing the risen Jesus, leaving aside the mention of their doubt or hesitation and thus any issues regarding a lack of will. Rather, Harrington presupposes believers who lack a proper knowledge of God's will regarding the nature of their ministry. Harrington also highlights the promise of Jesus' helping presence; thus he aims at empowering people who lack ability, who are powerless, or who may encounter resistance when attempting to make disciples.

Textual Choices

> *Most Significant Textual Features*: the figurative dimension of the text and its symbolic message; features located **in the text** (rather than in front or behind the text)
> *Methods*: history of traditions

Harrington focuses on features in the text that allude to the Septuagint (Greek translation of the Hebrew Bible, particularly Daniel 7:14) and to Jewish traditions. He emphasizes the figurative dimension of the text and its symbolic message, especially on Jesus as the Christ who is understood as "one like a human being" (the Son of Man). Daniel says, "I saw one like a human being coming with the clouds of heaven. . . . To him was given dominion and glory and kingship, that all peoples, nations, and languages should serve him. His dominion is an everlasting dominion that shall not pass away, and his kingship is one that shall never be destroyed" (Dan. 7:13-14). Jesus is given power and authority like that of the figure in Daniel ("To him was given dominion and glory and kingship" [Dan. 7:14*a*]). In Matthew, Jesus commands the disciples to make disciples of all nations, just as "all peoples" serve the one "like a human being" in Daniel (Dan. 7:14). Further, Matthew 28:20 refers to the continued presence of the risen Lord, just as Daniel refers to the ancient figure whose dominion is an everlasting dominion that shall not pass away, and his kingdom one that shall not be destroyed (Dan. 7:14*c*).

Theological Choices

Role of the Text as Scripture: Family Album (or Book of the Covenant) and Empowering Word (secondarily)
Theological Concepts: Mission, Christology, and Discipleship

Harrington understands the Great Commission as a divine mandate for Matthew's church as Christians are promised the presence of the risen Lord with them. Therefore, for Harrington, Scripture functions primarily as Family Album or Book of the Covenant. It establishes or reinforces one's identity and vocation as a member of the church (with the mission of making disciples), and it gives believers a true sense of relationship to others and to God. In this interpretation, Scripture has a secondary function as Empowering Word. The Scripture ensures believers that Jesus' helping presence will continue to guide them in their making disciples and manifesting God's kingdom.

This interpretation underscores two main theological concepts: Christology and discipleship. (1) Christology. For Harrington, the emphasis is on Jesus as universal Lord. These verses mark the beginning of a new chapter in the history of the Matthean community—"all the Jews who could be expected to come to . . . Jesus had already done so." The mission field changes from other Jews to Gentiles.[8] (2) Discipleship. Members of the church (disciples) understood the Great Commission as a divine mandate. The church and, individually, disciples are both commissioned and empowered by Jesus' supreme and universal authority to share their discipleship.[9] Being a member of the church (a disciple) requires one to make disciples through the continued ministry of Jesus. The most significant point for Harrington is not what the disciples teach, but who they teach (who *they* make disciples).

2) Musa W. Dube on the Great Commission[10]

The Teaching of Matthew 28:16-20 for Believers According to Dube

For Dube, the Great Commission instructs readers to disavow borders. Christians are commanded to *travel* to all nations with the pedagogical imperative to make disciples of all nations.[11] The passage neglects the issue of trespassing on someone else's property and gives Christians an unrestricted passport to enter all nations in obedience to their Lord, without any consultation whatsoever with the nations in questions (see Matt. 28:18*b*).[12] In addition, the text implies that Christians have a *duty* to teach all nations, without any suggestion that they must also in turn *learn* from all nations.[13] Ultimately, the Great Commission dismisses any relationship of reciprocity between Christian disciples and those nations being entered and discipled. One finds in this text an operative model of the disciples treating the nations as outsiders—as infants to be uplifted.[14]

Dube's Interpretive Choices

Theological Choices

> *Role of the Text as Scripture:* a negative role as an imperialistic text.
> *Theological Concepts*: mission, either imperialistic or approaching the other, as a dialogue partner.

For Dube, a biblical scholar in Botswana, the Great Commission (and the entire Bible) is viewed as an imperialistic text. The Bible in general, and the Great Commission in particular, has historically encouraged the Western Christian world to disavow borders, to enter any nation with authority, and to regard the occupants of such nations as untutored.[15] To liberate the biblical text from its imperialistic tradition requires readers of the Bible to read it in light of its historical employment, in dialogue with other canons and with other textual traditions (oral traditions, symbols, rituals, and so on). This reading will emphasize the life situations of real readers and interpret the text to confront such effects of the text as slavery, imperialism, colonialism, neocolonialism, anti-Semitism, homophobia, sexism, and racism in order to counteract texts or interpretations that perpetuate any of these forms of oppression.[16]

Members of the Western church view the Great Commission as a mission statement. The Western church is primarily a mission-oriented religion with a claim to absolute and universal truth. The Western church tradition, with its duty to travel, enter, and teach, fosters a socioeconomic ideology of imperialism that seeks to subjugate others while it creates in the process a relationship of dependency among tutors and the untutored (in Africa, for example). Dube's interpretation challenges the Western church to fulfill its mission statement by seeking others as dialogue partners, alternatively learning from them and teaching them.

Contextual Choices

> *Problem in the Interpreters' Life Context:* for Western churches, tendency to seek cultural, political, and economic domination of other nations; for African churches, being culturally, politically, and economically dominated.
>
> *Root Problem:* for Western churches, a lack of vision (resulting in the legitimating of domination); for African churches, a lack of vision (without which one cannot recognize the imperialism of the text and of Western Christianity).

For Dube, the teaching of this text addresses countries and churches who have employed the biblical text (particularly Matt. 28:18-19) to legitimate their cultural, political, and economic domination of other nations. The Great Commission is commonly understood to address readers who need legitimation (both initial and repeated) for their participation in the cultural, political, and economic domination of other nations. It provides for these believers a vision of the church's missionary (imperialist) duties a vision in which their missionary (imperialist) will, and their (wrong) knowledge of the way to pursue it, are rooted.

Dube says that this is a wrong vision because it devalues the reciprocity of knowledge. The Great Commission constitutes an imposition that undermines the autonomy and culture of the nations who are being made disciples.[17] As a consequence, Western Christians lack the (right) sort of vision to alert them to the intrinsic connection between imperialism and the Great Commission (or Christian texts in general). For Dube, a proper reading of a biblical text should accentuate not so much how the text interprets the life of the believer, but how the life of the believer must interpret the text. Western (and African) Christian communities are challenged to reevaluate the role of the biblical text in the devaluation of others' autonomy and cultures.

Textual Choices

> *Most Significant Textual Features:* **"in front of the text"**; how the text and its ideology are related to the socioeconomic and political situation of its readers.
>
> *Methods:* postcolonial criticism, voices from the margin.

Dube argues that Matthew 28:18-20 disavows borders on the historical context of Israel's struggle against the Roman Empire (the text imitates Roman universalist policy), the Hebrew Bible's account of the Exodus story (Israel takes land already occupied), and the historical circumstances of imperialism in the African context. Her reading is postcolonial, taking into account how marginalized people (in the Two-thirds World) are affected by the text and how they confront the text and its traditional interpretations through their own voices.[18] Their own voices reflect a different social and cultural perception of reality than those espoused by the biblical text or by dominant interpretations of the text.

3) Hal Freeman on the Great Commission[19]

The Teaching of Matthew 28:16-20 for Believers According to Freeman

The Great Commission is intended for all those who would follow Christ, and not just for the eleven disciples named in the text. It is universal in the sense that every disciple is to become a disciple-maker. Moreover, the Great Commission espouses the trinitarian view of God. Therefore, the theological perception of God as Father, Son, and Holy Spirit *must* be a part of the church's evangelical proclamations. The commands of Jesus supersede cultural values, and therefore in no cultural context may the demands of the gospel be truncated.[20] Finally, the Great Commission disavows borders. There is no place that is off limits to the power of the gospel. Jesus has been given universal power, and he has given his followers universal commission. This commission encompasses the whole gospel for the whole world.[21]

Freeman's Interpretive Choices

Contextual Choices

> *Problem in the Interpreters' Life Context*: Southern Baptist Christians who need to be encouraged to be missionaries. The problem is with the private lives of these individuals (whose minds need to be changed).
> *Root Problem*: lacking the will or the sense of responsibility to carry the gospel to all nations.

The seal of the Baptist university where Freeman teaches has the Greek text of a portion of Matthew 28:19, which translates into English as, "Make disciples of all nations."[22] With this statement, Freeman situates himself within the Southern Baptist denominational context. He addresses Southern Baptist Christians who lack the will or the sense of responsibility to carry the gospel to all nations. According to Freeman, the teachings of Jesus are universal and therefore apply to every person, regardless of cultural setting.

The root problem is therefore a lack of will to obey God's command, a universal moral standard. Comparison with Harrington and Dube's interpretation makes clear that, by contrast with them, Freeman highlights the ethical dimensions of the Great Commission, suggesting that Christians as individuals bear a moral standard that is universally appropriate. The Great Commission encourages Christians to fulfill their duty in spreading a gospel that is theologically trinitarian and ethically Christocentric to all *individuals* within every nation despite cultural and situational differences.

Theological Choices

> *Role of the Text as Scripture:* Canon.
> *Theological Concepts*: Mission and Christology

For Freeman, Scripture functions primarily as Canon. The Great Commission serves as a measure for assessing behavior and life. The Great Commission shapes the believers' moral lives so that the church may fulfill its mission. It also provides a means to recognize who does and does not belong to the church.

Freeman focuses his comments on two major theological themes: (1) Christology and (2) missiology.

1. *Christology.* Jesus' expression of the Trinitarian nature of God serves, for Freeman, as the central element of Matthew's christological emphasis. Baptism, as a characteristic of making disciples, requires that those baptized give public indication of a particular understanding of and relationship with God as God has been revealed by Jesus.[23] Freeman employs earlier Christian texts, including those from Paul,[24] to suggest that Jesus, in person and command, expresses the Trinitarian nature of God: "We have here one of the teachings that led to the later attempts to summarize doctrinally what Jesus said."[25]

2. *Missiology.* Members of the church through the centuries understood the Great Commission as essential to the Christian faith. For Freeman, this mission is to individuals. Matthew's usage of *ethne* (nations) and *terein* (to keep) grounds Freeman's mission emphasis. As for Matthew's use of "nations," he argues against the suggestion

that the disciples understand that their mission is to ethnic groups, and they must preserve the ethnic identity of each group.[26] Instead, Freeman writes, "the use of the masculine pronoun in the next clause *(autous)* means that the antecedent of 'them' cannot be the nations, since *ethne* is neuter. We would have expected *auto* otherwise. Thus, Matthew focuses the commission upon individuals, not nations."[27]

Textual Choices

> *Most Significant Textual Features*: **"in the text,"** symbolic; and **"behind the text,"** Window dimensions
> *Methods*: history of tradition and sociohistorical criticism.

Freeman's argument focuses on the *symbolic* dimension of the text. He maintains that the importance of the Great Commission to the Christian faith is consistent with "the prominent place it occupies in Matthew's gospel."[28] The commission provides the climactic conclusion of Jesus' ministry and is therefore a charge Matthew wanted the reader to remember. Moreover, the interpretation emphasizes the religious vision of the text created by its symbolic organization. The most significant features are those that refer to Jesus' authority in terms of Jewish traditions: Jesus as the new Moses, or as one greater than Moses (see Matt. 28:16, mountain imagery), and Jesus who is like the "one like a human being" (Son of Man) mentioned in Daniel 7:13-14. However, unlike Harrington's analysis that focuses on the similarities between Jesus and Daniel's ancient figure, Freeman highlights their differences. First, Jesus' power is presently realized, rather than expected in the future. Second, Jesus' kingdom reality rests neither on nationalist ideals nor on the ultimate submission of Israel's oppressors. Instead, in Matthew, "it is Jesus who rightly deserves submission, and his authority forms the basis for making disciples of, not executing vengeance upon, other nations" (see Matt. 7:18, 22).[29]

Freeman's argument focuses on the *window* dimension of the text, and thus the historical reality **behind the text**. Matthew 28:19 proves equally important to Freeman's analysis. Again, differing from Harrington's analysis, Freeman uses sociohistorical readings to argue that the disciples' mission to the Jews and the Gentiles continued simultaneously.[30] Freeman concludes, following the sociohistorical readings of Levine and Davies and Allison, "there is no evidence from Matthew that mission efforts to Jews should ever cease. . . . It is historically implausible that, in Matthew's time and place, there were no longer Christian missionaries to the Jew."[31]

4) George M. Soares-Prabhu, S.J., on the Great Commission[32]

The Teaching of Matthew 28:16-20 for Believers According to Soares-Prabhu

George Soares-Prabhu provides an exercise in intertextual study of two missionary commands: one Christian (Matt. 28:16-20) and the other Buddhist (Mahavagga 1.10-11.1). In this comparative analysis, George Soares-Prabhu uses the Buddhist text to illuminate the Christian text. See at the end of this chapter both this Buddhist text and a detailed summary of Soares-Prabhu's essay. Here it is enough to say that he draws out the similarities and differences, and the continuities and absences in these ancient texts and uses such a cross-religious reading to "question the traditional triumphalistic exegesis of the Matthean passage."[33] Because of Matthew's christological concentration, argues Soares-Prabhu, "the command tends to neglect, on the one hand, the dispositions of the missionaries sent by the Risen Lord, and on the other, the welfare of the people to whom the missionaries are sent."[34] Because of these oversights, the command can and has sometimes become the occasion for "a mission more preoccupied with aggrandizement of the missioner rather than the welfare of the missionized."[35] According to Soares-Prabhu, the comparison with the Buddhist text helps one arrive at a more developed interpretation of the mission command in Matthew. The intertextual analysis points to elements implicit in the Matthean text, which "could be overlooked in an over-focused, atomistic reading of the text."[36]

Soares-Prabhu's Interpretive Choices

Contextual Choices

> *Problem in the Interpreters' Life Context*: alienation faced by Asian readers of the Bible.
> *Root Problem*: an inadequate vision that engenders powerlessness; ideological alienation resulting from cultural clash.

This interpretation addresses the problem of the alienation experienced by Asian readers of the Bible. The Christianity practiced by 2 percent of its Asian people is a colonial Christianity whose doctrine, ritual, and ethics were developed in the West to respond to Western concerns and show little sensitivity to the entirely different sensibilities of Asian cultures.[37]

The problem of alienation (as an inadequate vision that engenders powerlessness) is couched in the contrasting understandings of the human being and ethical responsibilities presupposed by Western missionaries and the Asian missionized. Couched in the universal, context-free categories of Greek philosophy, "Christian ethics offers norms for behavior of persons construed as isolated self-sufficient individuals, in a culture where the human person is . . . experienced as connected to others."[38] This connectedness to others is reinforced by the perception of the individual as having permeable boundaries that allow a constant interchange of substance with others. The gap is further widened by the Asian sense of self as "we-self of the extended family or the caste rather than I-self of the West."[39] Finally, the process for spiritual growth seeks opposing ends in a traditional Christian and Asian self-understanding. "Christian spirituality proposes therapies for personal growth, in a Buddhist culture where the aim of religious discipline is not to strengthen the ego through the development of human potential or the proliferation of mental structures as unifiers of reality, but to dismantle them until only pure consciousness remains."[40] In light of the cultural disparities between the traditional Western Christian tradition and the non-Christian religiosity of Asia, Soares-Prabhu's teaching helps Asian Christian believers interpret the Bible by relating it "intertextually to Asia's living stories or Asia's religious texts."[41]

Textual Choices

> *Most Significant Textual Features*: Similarities and differences between Matthew 28:16-20 with the Buddhist text; features "in front of the text" (the features that enter in dialogue with the Buddhist text).
> *Methods*: Intertextual and intercontextual, postcolonial, and cultural criticisms.

Soares-Prabhu does not attempt to offer a universal biblical interpretive methodology for an Asian reader. He notes the cultural complexity of the Asian continent and therefore situates himself in Southern Asia. Nevertheless, he argues that the basic method of Asian exegesis should be the dialogical imagination—a method that relates the reader and text so that each interprets the other. He acknowledges that the sources used for such an analysis will take different forms at different times. Soares-Prabhu notes that the majority of Asian readers, employing the dialogical imagination as an interpretive tool, read the Bible in light of Asia's (1) overwhelming poverty and (2) multifaceted religiosity. Therefore, he offers two interconnected, but in no way exhaustive, strategies for biblical interpretation within an Asian context: The first of these will confront the Bible with Asian social concerns (stories of broken Asian humanity). The second will relate it to the texts of the great Asian religions. One can best interpret the Bible in Asia by "relating it intertextually to Asia's living stories or Asia's religious texts."[42] See at the end of this chapter his remarkable comparison of the parallel biblical and Asian scriptural texts.

Theological Choices

> *Role of the Text as Scripture*: Illuminating Word that empowers believers.
> *Theological Concepts*: Mission, liberation, and Christology.

For Soares-Prabhu, Scripture functions primarily as an illuminating Word (his frequent metaphor). Scripture—both the biblical text and Asian religious text—conjures a new reality in the present situation of otherwise confused believers and empowers them to struggle for the kingdom and God s justice.

Liberation and Christology surface as the two major themes in this interpretation of Christian mission.

1. *Liberation.* Soares-Prabhu employs liberation as a hermeneutical tool for comparing Asian religious texts with the Bible. According to Soares-Prabhu, interpreting the Bible in its postmodern Asian context can be liberating in at least three ways: (a) "the liberation of Asian religions, not excluding Christianity, from the precritical dogmatism [that] still plagues them and is a source of the malevolent fundamentalism that keeps erupting in so many parts of Asia today";[43] (b) "the prophetic critique of Asian reality that will foster the social liberation of Asia's marginalized people from their overwhelming poverty, social oppression, and patriarchy":[44] (c) a "spiritual liberation of the individual from the bondage of inordinate attachments, which is the primary goal of the non-Semitic religions of Asia."[45]

2. *Christology.* "The most striking feature of the mission command in Matthew is its Christological character. It is the Risen Lord who dominates the text from end to end."[46]

B) Holding a Second Roundtable on Matthew 28:16-20

Hold the second roundtable discussion, under the leadership of a member facilitator, following the guidelines provided in chapter 2. As usual, the goal of the second roundtable discussion is to help the members of the group identify and refine their theological and textual choices. Thus, each of the published interpretations should always be discussed in the process of comparing their interpretive choices with those of the participants. Each participant should also identify which of the four published interpretations is closer to his or her own—a good basis to refine one's interpretation. Thus, each participant should come to the roundtable after completing the following chart.

C) Sharing Results

Under the leadership of a member scribe, share the results of the second roundtable. In preparation for the third roundtable, it is particularly helpful for you to be aware if your interpretation is somewhat similar to one of the five published ones.

Interpreters' Contextual Choices	Daniel J. Harrington	Musa W. Dube	Hal Freeman	George M. Soares-Prabhu	Your Interpretation
1) Problem in the Interpreters' Life Context (see chap. 1, pp. 29-32)	1) the believers' lives in relationship with people of different religious convictions	1) for Western churches, a tendency to seek cultural, political, and economic domination of other nations; for African churches, being culturally, politically, and economically dominated	1) Southern Baptist Christians who need to be encouraged to be missionaries. The problem is with the private lives of these individuals (whose minds need to be changed)	1) alienation faced by Asian readers of the Bible	1)
2) Root Problem (see chap. 1, pp. 29-32)	2) a lack of knowledge of God's will and powerlessness	2) for Western churches, a lack of vision (resulting in the legitimating of domination); for African churches, a lack of vision (without which one cannot recognize the imperialism of the text and of Western Christianity)	2) lacking the will or the sense of responsibility to carry the gospel to all nations	2) an inadequate vision that engenders powerlessness; ideological alienation resulting from cultural clash	2)

Interpreters' Theological Choices	Daniel J. Harrington	Musa W. Dube	Hal Freeman	George M. Soares-Prabhu	Your Interpretation
1) Role of the Text as Scripture (see chap. 1, 27-28)	1) Family Album (or Book of the Covenant) and Empowering Word (secondarily)	1) a negative role as an imperialistic text	1) Canon	1) Illuminating Word that empowers believers	1)
2) Theological Concepts	2) Mission, Christology, and discipleship	2) Mission, either imperialistic or approaching the other as a dialogue partner	2) Mission and Christology	2) Mission, liberation, and Christology	2)

Interpreters' Textual Choices	Daniel J. Harrington	Musa W. Dube	Hal Freeman	George M. Soares-Prabhu	Your Interpretation
1) Most significant Textual Features (see chap. 2, pp. 54-57)	1) "in the text"; the figurative dimension of the text and its symbolic message	1) "in front of the text"; how the text and its ideology are related to the socioeconomic and political situation of its readers	1) "in the text," symbolic; and "behind the text," window dimensions	1) "in front of the text"; similarities and differences between Matthew 28:16-20 and the Buddhist text	1)
2) Methods (see chap. 2, pp. 54-57)	2) History of traditions	2) Postcolonial criticism, voices from the margin	2) History of tradition and sociohistorical criticism	2) Intertextual and intercontextual, postcolonial, and cultural criticisms	2)

III—Third Roundtable Discussion on Matthew 28:16-20

Four different interpretations of Matthew 28:16-20 are presented above. Each one is appropriately based on a significant aspect of the Bible passage. Each one is appropriately focused on certain theological concepts. Which one is "the best" reading? Which one is "the worst"? In order to assess the relative values of these four different interpretations, in a debate format, four participants should make a case for one of these interpretations as the best and one as the worst in the following concrete situation.[47]

Five missionaries are captured and imprisoned for teaching Christianity in a non-Christian country. The missionaries argue that they are divinely commissioned to seek out non-Christian nations and make Christian disciples of them. However, the authorities of the non-Christian nation consider the missionaries' actions both illegal and irreligious.

1. How would each of the readings address the respective attitudes of the missionaries and the non-Christian authorities?

2. In each case, how does the context she or he presupposed in her or his interpretation influence the author's conclusions about what is best for the missionaries in this situation.

3. In light of the apparent impasse between the missionaries and the government in the example above, which reading would best effect an equitable and just resolution to the problem? Why?

4. Which interpretation might further irritate the problem? Why?

5. How does the "best" interpretation lead to the glory of God and contribute to love of neighbor? How does the "worst" interpretation fail to do so?

Additional Resources: Soares-Prabhu's Comparison of Matthew 28:16-20 and a Buddhist Text, Mahavagga 1.10-11.1.

Soares-Prabhu's reading examines the similarity between the Matthean passage and the mission command given by the Buddha to his first followers, as narrated in the Mahavagga, a section of the Vinaya texts of the Pali Canon.[48]

Matthew 28:16-20

28:16—Now the *eleven disciples* went to Galilee, to the mountain to which Jesus had directed them.

17—When they saw him, they worshiped him, but some doubted.

A

18—*And Jesus came and said to them, "All authority in heaven and on earth has been given to me.*

(cf. Matt. 5:13-16)

B

19—*Go therefore and make disciples of all nations,*

baptizing them in the name of the Father and of the Son and of the Holy Spirit,

20—*and teaching them to obey everything that I have commanded you; (cf. Matt. 5:48)*

C

And remember, I am with you always, to the end of the age.

Mahavagga 1.10-11.1

1.10—At that time there were *sixty-one Arahats* in the world.

A

1.11—*The Lord said to the Bhikkus, "I am delivered, O Bhikkus, from all fetters, human and divine.*

You, O Bhikkus, are also delivered from all fetters, human and divine.

B

Go now, O Bhikkus, and wander for the profit of many, for the happiness of many, and out of compassion for the world, for the good, profit, and happiness of gods and human beings.

Let not two of you go the same way.

Preach, O Bhikkus, the dhamma, which is good in the beginning, good in the middle and good in the end, in the spirit and in the letter. Proclaim a consummate, perfect and pure life of holiness.

C

And I will go also, O Bhikkus, to Uruvela, Senanigama, in order to preach the dhamma.

The Context of the Mission Commands. "The mission command in Matthew concludes a coherent, carefully constructed narrative about Jesus . . . Its meticulously formulated verses bring Matthew's story of Jesus to a climactic end, and open out its significance to a future which reaches to the end of the age."[49] On the other hand, the Buddhist text is part of a "loose collection of traditions compiled as rules of disciple for the Buddhist monastic community. . . . The mission command here is one of several incidents in a crucial period of the life of the Enlightened One [Buddha], to which no special importance is given."[50] Soares-Prabhu suggests that Matthew 10 is the proper analogue for the Buddhist passage, but he also argues that Matthew 10 and 28 belong together. They are linked by Matthew's mythic understanding of time and by the paradigmatic role he assigns to the twelve disciples as representatives of the Christian community.[51] Ultimately, both mission commands serve the respective communities to which they were addressed and therefore can throw light on each other.

The Form of the Mission Commands. The form of the two mission commands is also similar. Both have the same tripartite structure. They (A) begin with a grounding of the mission in the authority of the sender. They then (B) proceed to spell out the mission, which in both cases involves teaching the communication of religious doctrine and praxis. And they both (C) conclude with a return to the sender, whose presence in one form or the other accompanies those who are sent.[52] Soares-Prabhu concludes that these form similar but independent mission commands and that mission commands from every cultural context conform to a basic structure. He therefore warns interpreters against the obsessive search for Jewish or Hellenistic models that have in fact dogged the study of Matthew's text.[53]

The Content of the Mission Commands. Thus far, much of Soares-Prabhu's analysis has highlighted points of similarity between the two mission commands. The content of the two commands, however, are strikingly different. Soares-Prabhu discusses five relevant points of comparison/contrast and illumination:

A) Comparison/contrast. While in Matthew, the mission command is grounded solely in the authority of Jesus ("All authority in heaven and on earth has been given to me"), in the Mahavagga, it is based not only on the liberation of the Buddha himself ("I am delivered from all fetters, human and divine"), but also, equally, on the similar liberation his followers have achieved ("You, O Bhikkus [Buddhist monks], are also delivered from all fetters, human and divine"). The Buddhist mission rests as much on the experience of the *bhikkus* he sends, as it does on the authority of the Buddha himself. It is because the *bhikkus* have, like the Buddha himself, attained enlightenment, that they can now, out of their own personal experience, proclaim the *dhamma*.[54] Matthew's mission command does not make explicit the need for such enlightenment (or conversion on the part of the missionary).

Illumination. Consequently, Matthew's mission command has often been taken as a military commissioning, which imposes the duty of proclaiming Christ on all true followers of Jesus. Reluctant Christians are whipped by guilt into a frenzy of mission.[55] However, the Buddhist text leads readers to read Matthew 28:16-20 in light of Matthew 10:42, 10:24-25, and 5:13-16. In these passages, the mission proceeds from a transforming encounter with the risen Lord, expressed as, but not really amounting to, a command. The Buddhist text thus reminds us that "the Christian mission, for all its Christological grounding, also presupposes the enlightenment of those who are sent."[56]

B) Comparison/contrast. Both mission commands include a summons to teach. The teaching of Jesus invites believers to be perfect as God is perfect (Matt. 5:48). The Buddha commands his disciples to preach the *dhamma*, the way to a perfect and pure life of holiness. Soares-Prabhu translates Christian perfection as *agape* (love) and Buddhist perfection as *nirvana* (freedom). Although the two concepts are different, there is a convergence between them. The Buddhist ideal of absolute freedom implies unlimited compassion, just as the Christian goal of unconditional love leads to perfect freedom. The ideal of the free and the compassionate person stands as the desired goal of both traditions.[57]

Illumination. The most significant and radical difference between the two traditions, possibly implied in the trinitarian formula for baptism that Matthew gives, is that a person becomes free and loving as part of a community of disciples among Christians, whereas he or she is liberated as an isolated individual in Buddhism.[58]

C) Comparison/contrast. Both mission commands aim at the ultimate liberation of humankind. In the Buddhist tradition, the aim is quite explicit. The monks are sent out for the benefit of the entire world. Mission for the Buddhist is an expression of that passionate desire for the welfare of all beings, which the Bhagavadgita (5.25; 12.4) posits as a significant attribute of the liberated human being.[59] The concern for the *welfare* of the nations or for the individuals to whom the disciples are being sent is absent from the Matthean text. However, the injunction (not found in the Buddhist text) to baptize them—that is, to bring the converts through a rite of initiation into a distinct social group—implies, of course, the welfare, indeed the supreme welfare, of the people baptized.[60]

Illumination. The priority to the welfare of the missionized group is not explicit in the Matthean passage and can easily be forgotten. Once again, the Buddhist intertext draws our attention to a dimension of the Christian text (all mission must be for the good, the profit, the happiness of the world and human beings) that is not explicitly expressed in it and can easily be overlooked.[61]

D) Comparison/contrast. Both mission commands are conscious of the universality and plurality of mission.

Illumination. The Buddhist tradition, however, extends its mission call beyond the human beings to the welfare of both creatures and nature. Though the Buddhist mission is even more universal than the Christian one, the Christian mission command is more "conscious of the unity of humankind than of national differences within it. It does not distinguish between nations, but between God and human beings."[62]

E) Comparison/contrast. Both commands end with a promise. "The promise is theologically significant in the mission command of Matthew, which promises the disciples the supportive presence of Jesus during their mission until the 'end of the age.'. . . These are wholly lacking in the mission command of the Buddha, who merely promises his *bhikkus* [Buddhist monks] to go out, just like him, to preach the *dhamma*. His presence fulfills at best an exemplary function."[63]

Illumination. The role of the Buddha in the text is the same as his monks —to preach the way of a pure and holy life. The Buddha neither empowers nor sustains the ministry of his disciples, as Jesus promises to do in Matthew 28:20.

Notes

1. Although the first and second roundtables may be held as a single round-table discussion, the preparation for each is nevertheless needed.

2. David Walker, *Appeal* (New York: Hill and Wang, 1995), 42-43.

3. We instinctively identified David Walker's contextual choices by comparing them with ours. Thus, from your different perspectives, you might want to emphasize different aspects of his interpretation.

4. Daniel J. Harrington, S.J., *The Gospel of Matthew* (Collegeville, Minn.: Liturgical Press, 1991).

5. Ibid., 2.

6. Ibid., 416.

7. Ibid.

8. Ibid.

9. Ibid., 416-17.

10. Musa W. Dube, "Go Therefore and Make Disciples of All Nations (Matt. 28:19a): A Postcolonial Perspective on Biblical Criticism and Pedagogy" in *Teaching the Bible,* ed. Fernando Segovia and Mary Ann Tolbert (Maryknoll, N.Y.: Orbis Books, 1998), 224-45.

11. Ibid., 224.

12. Ibid.

13. Ibid.

14. Ibid., 225.

15. Ibid., 233.

16. Ibid., 240.

17. Ibid., 230.

18. Scholars from non-Western countries prefer to refer to the "Third World" as the "Two-thirds World" to remind their readers that two-thirds of people and, indeed, two-thirds of the Christians are in the Third World.

19. Hal Freeman, "The Great Commission and the New Testament: An Exegesis of Matthew 28:16-20." *Southern Baptist Journal of Theology* 1, no. 4 (Winter 1997): 14-23.

20. Ibid., 20.

21. Ibid.

22. Ibid., 14.

23. Ibid., 18.

24. Freeman does not offer an analysis of any Pauline texts. Instead, he calls the readers' attention to Gordon Fee's "Christology and Pneumatology in Romans 8:9-11 and Elsewhere: Some Reflections on Paul as a Trinitarian," in *Jesus of Nazareth: Lord and Christ*, ed. Joel B. Green and Max Turner (Grand Rapids: Eerdmans, 1994), 312-31.

25. Freeman, "Great Commission," 18.

26. Ibid.

27. Ibid.

28. Ibid., 14.

29. Ibid., 17.

30. Ibid., 17-18.

31. Ibid., 18.

32. George M. Soares-Prabhu, S.J., "Two Mission Commands: An Interpretation of Matthew 28:16-20 in the light of a Buddhist Text," in *Voices from the Margins*, ed. R. S. Sugirtharajah (Maryknoll, N.Y.: Orbis Books, 1995), 319-39.

33. Ibid., 319.

34. Ibid., 333.

35. Ibid.

36. Ibid., 333-34.

37. Ibid., 323.

38. Ibid.

39. Ibid.

40. Ibid., 323-24.

41. Ibid., 325.

42. Ibid.

43. Ibid., 326.

44. Ibid.

45. Ibid.

46. Ibid., 332.

47. The moderator of the debate—usually the instructor or leader of the Bible study group—might want to intervene to make sure that each of the four interpretations is discussed.

48. Soares-Prabhu, "Two Mission Commands," 327. See Soares-Prabhu's essay for further description of these texts and their place in the Buddhist canon.

49. Ibid., 328.

50. Ibid., 329.

51. Ibid., 328.

52. Ibid., 329.
53. Ibid., 329-30.
54. Ibid., 330.
55. Ibid.
56. Ibid., 331.
57. Ibid.
58. Ibid.
59. Ibid., 331-32.
60. Ibid., 332.
61. Ibid.
62. Ibid. Compare with Freeman.
63. Ibid., 332-33.

CHAPTER 6

The Good News According to Matthew: Matthew 1:1–28:20

Introduction: Preparing for the Roundtables on Matthew 1–28

For the final set of roundtables, we consider the Gospel of Matthew as a whole. This is a much longer text than the Bible passages we considered so far. Yet you should be ready to prepare for, hold, and share the results of:

1. A first roundtable by preparing a contextual interpretation of the entire Gospel;

2. A second roundtable by entering in dialogue with the four authors of this book, who present their respective interpretations;

3. A third roundtable regarding the relative value of the different teachings of Matthew for believers, presented in the interpretations of the four authors. This will involve considering how these teachings apply in particular situations today.

I—First Roundtable on Matthew 1–28

With a Bible passage of this size, the procedure should obviously be somewhat adjusted. To begin with, we do not reproduce the text for you. You can find it in your own Bible, although we strongly recommend that you use two translations—including the New Revised Standard Version—to consult the second one regarding the passages that are particularly important to you.

As usual, you should prepare for the first roundtable. For this, you should formulate in writing a contextual interpretation of Matthew 1–28. Since you have already consulted several passages of Matthew, you are in a position to *select believers and their neighbors in a particular life context today* for which the Gospel of Matthew would have much needed "good news." Then, you should read the entire Gospel (it may take more than one sitting) with this question in mind: *What is the teaching of the Gospel of Matthew for believers in this specific life context.* Then, you will be ready to formulate this teaching (using the form on pp. 29-32 in chapter 1) and to identify the Gospel passages that are most significant.

Once again, remember that there is no learning if, through reading of the text, the readers/believers do not discover something new regarding the text itself or regarding their lives (viewed from the perspective of the text).

We expect the first and the second roundtable discussions will be held together. If not, you should follow the procedures for holding and sharing the results of the first roundtable in chapters 1 and 4.

II—Second Roundtable on Matthew 1–28

A) Preparing the Second Roundtable Discussion

In order to help you clarify your own contextual, theological, and textual choices in their contextual interpretations of Matthew 1–28, in this final chapter, we present four interpretations of the Gospel of Matthew as a whole. In each overview, the author has chosen different critical methods, addresses different questions to the text, and therefore regards one or another textual feature as most significant. This will become apparent as we underscore our respective textual choices. Although each author is a biblical scholar, each readily acknowledges that her or his textual choices also reflect contextual and theological choices. Each reads from and for a very different context. The authors are from different cultural settings and religious backgrounds. In brief, Revelation Velunta, a member of United Church of Christ in the Philippines, interprets the Gospel of

Matthew from and for his Filipino context. Justin Ukpong, a member of the Roman Catholic Church, interprets it from and for his Nigerian context. Monya Stubbs, a member of the African Methodist Episcopal Church, interprets it from her African American context and for Americans. Daniel Patte, a member of the Reformed Church of France, associated with the Presbyterian Church USA, interprets it from and for his European American context.

1) Revelation E. Velunta: A Filipino Reading of Matthew

The Life Context: Jeeps and Jeepneys

Biblical interpretation has privileged the centers of power within, behind, and in front of the text. Biblical studies in the Philippines have been a stronghold of colonial scholarship for over a century, especially among Protestant churches. Indigenous denominations refuse to become autonomous and continue to depend on their *mother* institutions in the United States or elsewhere in the First World. Church buildings and institutions are named after *benevolent* foreign church leaders and missionaries. Seminaries continue to have more foreign teachers (who are paid in dollars by foreign boards) than Filipinos (who are paid in pesos and, usually, significantly below the living wage). Libraries are filled with books written by European and American scholars and continue to receive donations of old books from the First World. Traditional historical-critical methods remain the key reading paradigm. Establishing what the Bible meant in the past is the first step toward discerning what it means today. Ways of interpreting the Bible that do not follow this so-called fundamental paradigm are labeled *eisegesis* (reading into the text) or reader-response. Filipino Protestants know more about Bible history and American history than their own history; and they read the Bible the way their colonial masters did and still do, because they have been socialized for generations that this is the correct way. Filipino social scientists call this collective condition of the Filipino psyche a colonial mentality. Historian Renato Constantino traces it to the systematic mis-education of Filipinos. Theologian Eleazar Fernandez argues that the Philippines can still be called a "mental colony" of the United States of America. Biblical studies in the Philippines today exemplifies his claim.

But side by side with this "reading-the-Bible-the-way-our-masters-do" is a wealth of Filipino literature, practices, and reading strategies that engage the Bible in unexpected ways. I call these interpretations models of *jeepney* hermeneutics. The *jeepney* is the most popular mode of public transportation in the Philippines. It is an excellent example of the

Filipinization of an American icon, the military jeep. It is also, as I will argue, one very powerful metaphor for Filipinos' engagement with another icon, the Bible, offering a range of strategies to decolonize biblical studies.

The U.S. Army, back in 1940, required an all-terrain reconnaissance, go-anywhere, vehicle that seated three and had a mount for a 30-caliber machine gun. Filipinos have turned this military vehicle into a sort of mini-bus that can accommodate about twenty people. There are those who look at a jeepney and call it Frankenstein's monster. There are others who see it as a "Filipino home on wheels," complete with an altar. The military jeep was, and still is, a sort of imperializing text. A jeepney resists this text.

Theological Issues Arising from This Life Context: Reading Matthew Inside a Jeepney

Interpretation, by definition, is always perspectival and particular. In other words, everything—including the supposedly objective historical-critical method—is reader-response. It is implicitly a scriptural reading that needs to be assessed by scriptural criticism. This interpretation of Matthew as an imperializing text presupposes the reality of an empire (the Roman Empire—the contemporary empire perceived as a reality by the biblical colonized people) as a backdrop to the construction of the narrative. Many Filipinos employ a similar assumption when engaging Filipino resistance literature: for example, Jose Rizal's *Noli Me Tangere* and *El Filibusterismo*, Francisco Baltazar's *Florante at Laura*, and Carlos Bulosan's *America Is in the Heart*. This interpretation does not equate the Gospel of Matthew with historical facts. What it does is argue that the Gospel is constructed and framed by a particular historical setting, in this case the Roman imperial occupation.[1] Anticolonialist Frantz Fanon and educator Paolo Freire show that dynamics leading to literary production exist not only between the colonizer and the colonized, but also between various interest groups of the colonized, some of which try to gain power to define national cultural identity, as well as to compete for the attention of their collective oppressor. The interpretation below argues that Matthew is not rejecting Roman imperialism, but seeking its favor, or at least condoning it.

This interpretation also presupposes resistance, as reflected in what activist Salud Algabre and historian Reynaldo Ileto call "little traditions." Algabre and Ileto memorialize all those resistance fighters who have been victimized by the violence of institutionalized forgetting, a fate most of the unnamed children in Matthew share.

Textual and Theological Choices: Matthew, Empire, and the Pais

New Testament scholar Musa Dube posits the following questions in order to measure whether Matthew is an imperializing text: Does the text offer an explicit stance for or against Roman imperialism? Does the narrative encourage travel to distant and inhabited lands, and how does it justify such travel? How does the narrative present those who are different from the main characters? Is there dialogue and liberating interdependence between the main characters and "others"? Or is there condemnation and replacement of all that is foreign and other? Is the celebration of difference authentic or mere tokenism? Does the text present relationships of subordination and domination? How does it represent them?

Using these questions to analyze Matthew and its effects upon its readers, Dube concludes that the author's stance toward the imperial powers presents imperial rule and its agents as holy and acceptable. Matthew's Jesus is politically unsubversive and encourages travel to distant and inhabited lands. Matthew's positive presentation of the Empire and the decision to take the word to the nations (Matt. 28:16-20) is born within and as a result of stiff competition for power over the crowds (Israel) and the favor of the Empire. Matthew's mission to the nations embodies imperialistic values and strategies. Matthew does not seek relationships of liberating interdependence among nations, cultures, and genders. Rather, this Gospel upholds the superiority of some races and relegates other races to inferiority. Matthew represents gender relationships as relationships of subordination and domination by featuring the Canaanite woman (15:21-28) and the centurion (8:5-13) in contrasting stories, which foreshadows the mission to the nations. Matthew's presentation of Pilate, his wife, and the Roman soldiers at the trial, death, and resurrection of Jesus shows a clear-cut pro-empire position (27:1–28:15).

The encounter between the centurion and Jesus, according to Dube, particularly highlights Matthew's stance toward the Empire. Both men are presented as having authority to effect things simply by the power of their words (Matt. 8:8-9). The comparison of Jesus' authority with that of the centurion's has the effect of sanctifying the imperial power. Jesus pronounces the centurion's faith greater than the faith of everyone in Israel (Matt. 8:10), a statement that contrasts the imperial agent with the colonized and exalts his righteousness above theirs. The passage casts imperial officials as holier and predicts that they, and other groups, will have more power (in the kingdom of God). Such characterization not only disguises what imperial agents represent—institutions of exploitation and oppression—but also pronounces imperialism holy and acceptable. A quick survey of the history of the interpretation of Matthew and centuries of Western colonization—euphemistically called "civilizing missions"—in Asia, Africa, and Latin America shows that most interpreters followed the Gospel's imperial rhetoric.

The centurion is to Matthew as the 30-caliber machine gun mount is to the military jeep. To read Matthew inside a jeepney is to celebrate the fact that the first thing Filipinos did in their transformation of the military jeep was to rid it of that machine gun mount. To read Matthew inside a jeepney is to remove our gaze from the centurion—and even Jesus, who mimics the centurion—and focus it on someone else. I suggest focusing our attention on the servant (*pais* in Greek) of 8:5-13.

The *pais*, whether translated son, daughter, girl, boy, servant, slave, or sex slave, is a child. He or she serves to remind flesh and blood readers that the reality of empire—in varying forms and degrees—is experienced by children and by those who are treated as children. Political sociologist Ashis Nandy draws attention to the way the colonized are viewed as children by the colonizers.[2]

Fred Atkinson, the first American General Superintendent of Education in the Philippines, inaugurated more than a century of racist public education in the islands when he remarked that "the Filipino people, taken as a body, are children and childlike, do not know what is best for them. . . . By the very fact of our superiority of civilization and our greater capacity for industrial activity we are bound to exercise over them a profound social influence."[3]

The *pais* reminds flesh and blood readers that children's oppression—of varying forms and degrees—is written in the text because, despite the rhetoric that God's reign is for children (Matt. 19:14), no child is ever named—except Jesus—or is given a voice in the gospel—except Herodias's daughter, who says what her mother tells her to say. Like the Canaanite woman's daughter (15:21-28) and the *pais*, Herodias's daughter serves only as a medium through which competing discourses present their claims. The girl falls prey to manipulation by her mother and by Herod. We don't even get to hear the cries of the children who are massacred in 2:18, only their mothers' cries. Children are the primary victims of Matthew's "culture of silence."

Look at how the *pais* is described in Greek: *ho pais mou*, "the servant who is mine." That child's body is under somebody else's control—whether it's his father, his owner, or, as I have argued elsewhere, his pedophile. The centurion's act on the *pais*'s behalf emphasizes the latter's marginalization. As far as Matthew is concerned, the *pais* cannot speak or seek his own healing. Yet, because that child is "paralyzed," albeit momentarily, he also paralyzes his owner, who must seek help from Jesus. The child also interrupts the goings and the comings of the centurion's soldiers, since the centurion is not with them to give them orders (Matt. 8:9). Thus, with his paralysis, the child also interrupts the imperial expansion. Throughout the Gospel, characters come and go, borders are crossed: magi from the East come seeking the king of the Jews (2:1-12); Joseph and his family flee into Egypt (2:13-15); Herod sends his death squads to Bethlehem to murder children (2:16-18); Joseph and his family go to Nazareth, from Egypt (2:19-23); Jesus goes to John the baptizer and is led by the Spirit into the wilderness (3:1–4:11); Jesus leaves Nazareth and makes his home in Capernaum (4:12); the centurion comes to Jesus and the latter is convinced of the imperial authority that effects goings and comings, travel to distant lands, and control at a distance (8:5-13). The disciples are systematically prepared for their commissioning (10:1-42); the Canaanite woman comes to Jesus (15:21-28); the heavy-laden come to Jesus (11:28). Jesus eventually sends out his disciples (28:16-20). Everyone in the story moves, except the *pais* in Matthew 8:5-13. Yes, even for a brief moment, the *pais* revels in the space her paralysis brings. For about eight short verses in the very long chapter 28 of the Gospel of Matthew, the *pais* is free of the centurion. The colonized is free of her colonizer.

Revisiting the Life Context: The Pais, Jeepneys, and Filipinos

The majority of Filipinos remain colonized subjects, a part of a mental colony. Migrant Filipina domestic workers, numbering over 7 million, are the global servants of late capitalism. Tens of millions find themselves squatters in their own homeland. Those who have opted for "the Promise Land"—the United States—find themselves treated as second-class citizens. Yet, despite all this colonization, they have always resisted. The *jeepney* is the best-known symbol of resistance and decolonization for Filipinos. Now, because of the Gospel, they have another symbol, the *pais* who disrupts imperial progress, even if only briefly, in the Gospel of Matthew.

2) Justin Ukpong, Matthew, and HIV/AIDS in Sub-Saharan Africa: God Is in Solidarity with Us in Our Suffering

The Life Context

Since it was diagnosed in the 1980s, HIV/AIDS has continued to ravage the human population. Global statistics show that at the end of 1999, 34.3 million adults and children were living with it, and 2.8 million had died of it; and of these 24.5 million and 2.2 million, respectively, came from sub-Saharan Africa.[4] Apart from cultural factors such as taboo, witchcraft, and stigma, the prevalence of AIDS in Africa is strongly associated with poverty. Fighting it therefore requires action at different levels—economic, political, social, cultural, and religious—with a focus that embraces education, prevention, and treatment. Because AIDS is as yet incurable, an important aspect of such action is helping Christians cope with AIDS in the light of the Word of God.

Theological Issues Arising from This Life Context

Christian faith teaches that we have a God who is good and loving. Many African Christians therefore raise questions about God in the situation of anguish and suffering caused by AIDS; some even think that God sends AIDS as a punishment for sin. However, Matthew's Gospel gives a different perspective on God and human suffering. Matthew presents Jesus as the manifestation of God's saving presence in the world, and his ministry as the inauguration of God's rule on earth. In the cultures of Matthew's time, sickness was commonly explained as a result of sin (cf. Matt. 9:1-2; John 9:1-2).[5] Matthew, however, understands God's rule on earth as God's empowering presence to reverse the course of our suffering. Suffering and death therefore do not have the last word. God does. The real question is not why we suffer, but how we should respond to suffering.

Textual Choices

What follows is a sociopolitical and religious interpretation of Matthew's Gospel, asking the following questions:[6] Does God abandon people because of their sin? What is the message of the Gospel about suffering? How does the Gospel present Jesus and his kingdom message in relation to human suffering? How do we respond to suffering? The interpretation will focus on Matthew's introduction to Jesus' ministry (Matthew 1–4), the Sermon on the Mount (5–7), the healing miracles (8–9, 12, 14–15, 17, 20), and the passion and resurrection narratives (27–28).

Introduction to Jesus' Ministry (Matthew 1–4)

Matthew introduces Jesus' ministry by recounting his ancestry, birth, baptism, and temptation in the desert. He traces Jesus' ancestry (Matt. 1:1-17) from Abraham, whose descendants were God's people and mediators of God's blessings to humanity (Gen. 12:1-3), through David, to whose heirs God had promised an eternal kingship (2 Sam. 7:11-17). From the beginning, Matthew tells us that God is in solidarity with God's people, even in their suffering and in spite of their sins.

Matthew's reference to Jesus as the "son of David" calls to mind the loss of the Davidic reign during the Babylonian exile (2 Kings 25) and points to the birth of Jesus as the restoration of that reign. Many times the chosen people sinned against God. So did King David himself (2 Sam. 11–12) and many others mentioned in the genealogy. The four women included in the genealogy—Tamar, Rahab, Ruth, and Solomon's mother (Bathsheba)—were mothers of people in Jesus' ancestry, who were born out of unions that were far from blameless. All this indicates Jesus' solidarity with people who were not perfect. Matthew shows that in spite of their sins, God did not abandon them or the rest of humanity, to whom they were designated mediators of God's blessings.

The promised child has the name "Jesus," which means "the one to save his people from their sins" (Matt.1:21), and "Emmanuel," "God with us" (1:23). These names have significance for the mission of the child: Jesus is the savior who will manifest God's saving presence in the world. In Jesus, the God we cannot see comes among us in a visible form to empower and save us. His birth was greeted with violence and suffering. His birth brought the slaughter of innocent children (2:16-18). Jesus and his family became refugees, fleeing into Egypt. With that journey, Jesus came to share a common lot with his Israelite ancestors, who also sojourned in Egypt (Gen. 46). With that journey, too, he came to share the plight of numerous refugees all over the world today. That Jesus shared all this suffering from his birth indicates that human suffering is a principal focus of his saving mission.

Those who received John's baptism had accepted John's proclamation of repentance and his vision of God's reign on earth (Matt. 3:5-8). Jesus' baptism demonstrates his solidarity with these Israelites (3:13-15).[7] The declaration that Jesus is the Son of God (3:17) authenticates this solidarity and interprets it as God's saving action. Jesus' baptism therefore shows that God acts to save in solidarity with us.

In the temptation story (Matt. 4:1-11), Jesus resists the devil and affirms his loyalty and commitment to God. Jesus' temptation may be compared to that of Eve (Gen. 3:1-6). Eve entered into conversation with the tempter and was overcome; Jesus dismissed each temptation as it was presented. Human beings are no strangers to temptation or the anguish that accompanies it. In this story, Matthew points to God's solidarity with us when tempted. He also provides a model of response to temptation.

The Beatitudes (Matt. 5:3-12)

In the mountain discourse (Matthew 5–7), Matthew gathers together Jesus' teachings that illustrate the life under God's reign and that reveal the inner characteristics of this reign. A new vision of life that is different from and often contrary to the contemporary one is presented. What does this vision reveal about God's reign and human suffering?

The beatitudes are promises of the blessings of God's reign on earth, and their focus is on situations of human suffering.[8] Being "poor in spirit" (Matt. 5:3) refers to situations of deprivation, not only economic and social, but also, and particularly, in the innermost being, the spirit. The "poor in spirit" are dehumanized and rendered nonpersons.[9] The second beatitude concerns situations of suffering that are accompanied with mourning (5:4). The third beatitude, "blessed are the meek" (5:5), concerns those who suffer at the hands of the wicked, without retaliating. They trust in God's power to save them (Ps. 37). The situations of oppression and injustice that call for God's vindication are the focus of the fourth beatitude (Matt. 5:6). As in our contemporary world, such situations were not uncommon in Palestine at the time of Jesus.[10] The arrival of God's reign in Jesus means the reversal of all these situations. Those who respond to suffering with works of mercy (Matt. 5:7) and by brokering peace (Matt. 5:9), and those who live a life of integrity without bringing suffering on others (the "pure in heart" in Matthew 5:8) are the objects of God's favor. In the next three beatitudes, they act like God in seeking to eliminate suffering. Those who suffer persecution receive God's blessing in the last two beatitudes (Matt. 5:10-12).

Beyond the Beatitudes

Although the beatitudes are about the reversal of situations of suffering, the rest of the discourse deals with human suffering under God's reign. Living under God's reign demands entrance through a difficult gate (Matt. 7:13-14), a higher standard of justice than the prevalent one (Matt. 5:39-48), contentment with the basic necessities of life (Matt. 6:10; 10:9-10), and choosing between one's own family and Jesus (Matt. 10:37-39). This last was particularly difficult in Palestine, where family ties were very strong.[11] This teaching demands that disciples follow Jesus' way of the cross (Matt. 10:38; 11:30; 16:24). Accepting the kingdom, with the suffering this entails, assures that we are empowered by Jesus. In Jesus we will "find" our lives and our burdens are made light (Matt. 11:30).

The Healing Miracles (Matt. 8–9; 12; 14; 15; 17; 20)

Sickness brings physical and emotional suffering and affects the sick persons themselves, their families, and caregivers. One person's sickness means suffering for many. In the healing miracles, Matthew shows that God is concerned to take away human suffering.

Of the seventeen miracles of Jesus described in Matthew's Gospel, fourteen are healing miracles. Only three—the calming of the storm (Matt. 8:23-27) and the two miracles of loaves (Matt. 14:13-21 and 15:32-39)—are not healing related. This demonstrates how important deliverance from human suffering was for Jesus' ministry. In these miracles Matthew presents Jesus as the suffering servant of God (Isa. 53:4) who has come to take on himself humanity's sickness and disease (Matt. 8:17). Jesus is the manifestation of God's saving presence in the world. In addition to the narrated miracles, Matthew punctuates his stories of Jesus' healings with the affirmation that Jesus healed all types of diseases (Matt. 4:23-25; 8:16-17; 14:34-36; 15:29-31) in order to indicate the comprehensive nature of God's saving involvement in human suffering. According to Matthew, God is involved in every kind of human suffering.

Matthew describes six different categories of healing—demon related (five instances); paralysis (three instances); blindness (two instances); and one instance each of leprosy, hemorrhage, and fever; and the raising of a dead person to life. Exorcism, with the highest number of instances, is an important focus of Jesus' healing ministry. The inauguration of God's reign on earth must mean the destruction of the devil's power (Matt. 9:32-34; 12:22-32). Jesus was the manifestation of God's power in the human community to overcome the devil's power, before which human beings were powerless.

Jesus' exercise of the power to forgive sin (Matt. 9:1-8), which was reserved to God alone (Mark 2:6-7; Matt. 9:3, 6), demonstrates that God's reign in the world had begun to be realized in Jesus. The miracles were also concrete realizations of the beatitudes that concerned the arrival of God's reign. Demoniacs and lepers are good examples of "the poor in spirit" (Matt. 5:3). The demoniac at Gadara lived in the cemetery (Matt. 8:28-34). He could not share the same physical space with the rest of the community. Lepers, too, had to live outside the community until they were healed (Lev. 13:1-59, 14:2-32; Num. 5:1-4). Their poverty went beyond the level of material well-being to their innermost being, their self-worth as persons, for they were treated as nonpersons. When they were healed, their full humanity was restored. They were treated as persons and reintegrated into the community. The second beatitude speaks of comfort for those who mourn (Matt. 5:4). Death and sickness put people in a situation of mourning. The raising of the synagogue official's dead daughter to life and the other healing miracles of Jesus (Matt. 9:18-19; 23-26) brought comfort to those in situations of mourning. What these miracles indicate is that God's reign had already arrived in Jesus, though that reign still awaits complete fulfillment at the end time.

Passion and Resurrection Narratives (Matt. 26–28)

In the passion, death, and resurrection narratives, Matthew presents the culmination of God's involvement in human suffering and offers a Christian approach to suffering. He tells us that Jesus performed his ministry in the full consciousness that he would suffer and die in Jerusalem on account of that ministry. Jesus made this known to his disciples on three occasions during his ministry (Matt. 16:21-23; 17:22-23; 20:17-19), and while they were in Jerusalem (Matt. 21–25, 26:1-2; 26:12). Yet he did not go into Jerusalem secretly, but openly, with fanfare fully claiming the messianic mission for which he was to die (Matt. 21:1-11).

Though he knew that his fellow Jewish religious officials were planning to kill him, he taught publicly and fearlessly in the temple, challenging their misguided use of authority. He dislodged the sellers and buyers at the temple precincts in defiance of the authority of these religious leaders (Matt. 21:12-17). He told them in parables that God would take away their preferential position and give it to others if they did not repent (Matt. 21:33-46; 22:1-14; 24; 25:1-13). He indicted the scribes and Pharisees for their hypocrisy and predicted the destruction of the Temple (Matt. 23:1-39; 24:1-3). The lesson here is clear: Those who follow Jesus must not be intimidated by the prospect of suffering. They must face suffering squarely and trust in God, who will empower them to turn it into an instrument of salvation.

The religious leaders had planned to have Jesus killed because of the messianic claims of both his teachings and his actions (Matt. 21:23-27, 45-46; 26:3-5). At one point, they planned to entrap him to say something about payment of tribute to Caesar that would incriminate him with the Roman authorities or the Mosaic Law (Matt. 22:15-40). When this failed, they confronted him head-on. They arrested, tried, and sentenced him to death. At Pilate's orders, he was crucified.

However, Jesus' crucifixion was not the end of the story. Jesus rose from death and appeared to his followers, sending them to preach the very good news that he had preached, this time not only in Palestine, but all over the world (Matt. 28:16-20). In response to this story, Paul declared:

> Death has been swallowed up in victory
> Where, O death, is your victory?
> Where, O death, is your sting? (1 Cor. 15:54b-55)

With the inauguration of God's reign by Jesus, suffering and death are no longer the last word. God, who has granted victory over them, has the final say.

Revisiting the Life Context: Christian Response to Suffering

How do we respond to the suffering brought about by the AIDS epidemic? At different points in his Gospel, Matthew indicates what a Christian response to suffering should be. One theme stands out clearly: We must not be passive sufferers. We must actively confront suffering because God is with us in our suffering to empower us and reverse the course of suffering. We must face suffering with determination. We must not allow it to crush us; we must not allow suffering to "overtake" us, but rather should anticipate it, prepare for it, and "look" it in the face when it comes. We overcome it by relying on God's power acting in us.

3) Monya A. Stubbs: Matthew's Challenge to Status Quo Authority

The Life Context

"You're on Your Own, Baby" reads the cover of a January 2002 issue of *Time* magazine. The cover title and feature articles address the plight of American citizens (and many others around the world) at the dawn of the twenty-first century.[12] Now, arguably, the authority governing our existence is more economic than religious or political. Based on the presumption that "choice" is a cornerstone of American culture, the magazine's articles suggest that variety is a "measure of American freedom and a source of our innovation and prosperity."[13] On the other hand, the authors note the overwhelming and ultimately dangerous effect on American citizens as society imposes "more and more responsibility for vital and complex decisions about our savings for college and retirement, our family's health care and the providers of our utilities."[14] Freedom of choice comes with a certain level of responsibility, but, as these articles point out, making informed decisions about such critical issues requires so much research and area-specific knowledge that many people feel overwhelmed. Adding to this bewilderment, these authors reach the debasing conclusion that many of the "professionals on whom we would like to rely for guidance are proving untrustworthy and even corrupt."[15] The professionals on whom we rely are often paid more to offer us shaky and unhealthy choices than to provide us with solid, sensible ones. These *Time* articles analyze this dilemma as a crisis that confronts Americans as consumers. The *Time* editors assume that the whole of our existence is controlled by the market and by those who have the time and skills to acquire and master the information needed to manipulate the market. We are reminded that "when money is involved, we are truly on our own."[16]

Theological Issues Arising from This Life Context

How does the Gospel of Matthew address the social needs of justice and love in relation to authority in society? How does Matthew address the crisis in authority? Driven by the goal of economic advancement, instead of a concern for the betterment of the human condition, our civic and corporate leaders often employ their social authority against citizens rather than in their service. The *Time* authors deduce a certain relationship between humanity and the economic structure. They assume that human beings interact with one another as if humanity is embedded in the economy, instead of using economic structures as tools for managing human needs.

The Gospel of Matthew also speaks about a crisis of leadership.[17] Matthew asserts the authority of Jesus and his followers while discounting the authority of their textual enemies, the traditional Jewish leadership (Pharisees, scribes, priests and elders; see Matt. 9:11; 9:34; 12:1-14; 12:24-32; 23). Matthew discredits the authority of the scribes and Pharisees. Their authority is associated with dominance and prestige. They use their positions to "lord" over and burden the masses (Matt. 23:1-7). According to Matthew, true authority rests in persons and institutions that utilize power to effect change for the better in the lives of others (Matt. 8:1–9:38; 10:1-8). In Matthew, the interpretation and priority of the law in the community's life are the primary points of contention between Jesus (and his followers) and the traditional Jewish leadership. Yet it is not the role of law or its authority in the life of the community that Matthew challenges (Matt. 5:17). Rather, the evangelist objects to those who exalt the law without regard for the needs of people. By comparison, our present-day economic structures often take priority over human welfare. Matthew argued that traditional Jewish leadership placed humanity at the mercy of the law (Matt. 12:1-14). In so doing, they made the law a tool of spiritual and physical oppression, instead of an expression of God's righteousness and love for the people.

Texual Choices: Matthew's Passages About Authority

Louis Althusser explains ideology in the sense that people are always already subject to the normative ideas or values that lie at the roots of particular societies. He maintains that ideology is a "representation of the imaginary relationship of individuals to their real conditions of existence."[18] Ideology is a construct of the relationship with one's condition of existence. The ideological lens of authority helps make sense of the text of Matthew for the North American contemporary context. Focusing on Matthew's characterization of authority and its effect on human relationships shapes the following analysis of the Gospel.

Matthew uses the Greek term *exousia* (authority) on six different occasions in his Gospel (Matt. 7:29, 8:9, 9:6, 9:8, 10:1, and 21:23). In Matthew 8:9 the centurion recognizes his own authority as inadequate, and therefore Jesus calls him a person of great faith. The centurion's authority reflects the power of one person (or group, or institution) to "legitimately" dominate another. Matthew rejects this type of power. Matthew 9:6 and 9:8 speak of Jesus' authority. In response to the scribes' accusation of blasphemy for forgiving the sins of a paralytic, Jesus states, "But so that you may know that the Son of Man has *exousia* [authority] on earth to forgive sins. . . . 'Stand up, take your bed and go to your home' " (Matt. 9:6). For Matthew, authority is not the power of one person over others, to command them to serve the personal interests of the strong. Instead, Jesus defines authority as serving the paralytic. In 9:8, the crowd responds with awe, glorifying God, "who had given such *exousia* [authority] to human beings." The crowd glorified God because God sanctions human beings (for example, Jesus as the Son of Man) not to dominate others and grants them authority to enter into relationship with those in need, to create a new reality for the afflicted. In Matthew 10:1, Jesus gives his disciples *exousia* [authority] over "unclean spirits, to cast them out, and to cure every disease and every sickness." The disciples are granted authority over circumstances that prohibit human beings from living productive and healthy lives. Jesus' conversation regarding his authority with the chief priests and the elders in Matthew 21:23-28 introduces the scathing attacks that he launches against them, and also against the Pharisees, in the form of parables regarding their unwillingness to do the work of God (see Matt. 21:33-46).

Finally, Matthew 7:28-29 marks the crowd's response to Jesus' Sermon on the Mount: "Now when Jesus had finished saying these things, the crowds were astounded at his teaching, for he taught them as one having *exousia* [authority], and not as their scribes." The scribes lack the influence to affect the thinking, commitments, and actions of the people. The reason for the crowds' reaction lies in the previous verses (Matt. 7:24-26), in which Jesus notes that speaking and hearing the word of God is insufficient. Only those who act upon or do *(poiei)* these words fulfill the will of God and thus have authority. The scribes do not teach with authority because they do not act with authority. This is clear, too, from Matthew 23:1-4:

> Then Jesus said to the crowds and to his disciples, "The scribes and the Pharisees sit on Moses' seat; therefore, do whatever they teach you and follow it; but do not do as they do, for they do not practice what they teach. They tie up heavy burdens, hard to bear, and lay them on the shoulders of others; but they themselves are unwilling to lift a finger to move them."

Jesus acknowledges that the scribes and Pharisees are authoritative (in the sense that authority refers to leadership that is culturally legitimated they sit on Moses seat). But Matthew is not satisfied with normative leadership. He defines legitimate authority as possession of both the ability and the will to serve those suffering from burdens, which are often unjust or unnecessary.

"And Behold a Leper" (Matt. 8:1-4): Matthew's Subversive Appropriation of the Leper

Matthew 7:29 and its comparison of Jesus' authority with that of the scribes is a prelude to Jesus' encounter with the leper. Matthew 8:1-4 bridges the Gospel's portrayal of Jesus as a teacher who speaks the Word of God and a healer who acts on the Word of God. This passage exposes the fullness of Matthew's definition of authority as one's willingness to effect change for the better in the life of the dispossessed. This story foreshadows Jesus' later polemic against those in leadership positions. Yet to read Matthew through the lens of 8:1-4 as a challenge to status quo authority is to look first at the leper, rather than at Jesus. The leper comes to Matthew with a literary reputation in the tradition as a subversive character, as one who has challenged or will challenge authority figures (see Num. 12:1-16; 2 Kings 5:15-27; 2 Chron. 26:16-21; Exod. 4; Job 1). Matthew is also aware that the leper is historically on the lowest rung of the social ladder (see Lev. 13:45-46; Num. 12:12; Matt. 10:8; 11:5).[19] The leper who meets Jesus on the outskirts of Capernaum represents a combination of these traditions.

Portraying the leper as a person in need of Jesus' help, though neither timid nor impotent, Matthew omits Mark's references both to the emotions of Jesus and to the leper. Matthew's leper does not incite Jesus' compassion (Matt. 8:2, compare Mark 1:41), nor does he approach Jesus begging and kneeling (compare Mark 1:40). Instead, the leper supports Matthew's critique against traditional Jewish leadership as exploiting its position of authority by saying, "Lord if you are willing, you are able to cleanse me." The leper's emphasis rests on Jesus' will (see Matt. 8:2), rather than on his power. Confident in Jesus' ability, the leper insists that Jesus distinguish himself from traditional authority through a willingness to serve (compared with the unwillingness of traditional authority in Matthew 23).

After assuring the leper of his desire to cleanse him, Jesus touches him and commands that he "be made clean" (Matt. 8:3). Jesus' touch is worth noting for two reasons. First, touching a leper causes ritual contagion (Lev. 5:3);[20] and second, Jesus sometimes heals people without touching them (for example, Matt. 8:8-13). Why does Jesus touch the leper in order to cleanse him? When viewed from Matthew's definition of authority, Jesus' decision to touch the leper represents symbolic action. It is an "action whose fundamental significance, indeed power, lies relative to the symbolic order (ideology) in which it occurred."[21] Interpreted within the ideological world of the biblical purity codes, Jesus' touch takes on messianic significance. Jesus welcomes the state of uncleanness that comes with touching a leper. He humbles himself and is therefore exalted (23:12). He enters as "Lord" in a relationship with the leper (8:2). However, through his touch, Jesus shifts his ideological stance, collapsing the boundaries between clean and unclean persons. By the end of chapter 8, Matthew's characterization of Jesus moves from "Lord" to "suffering servant" (Matt. 8:17, quoting Isa. 53:4)—the one who takes infirmities and bears diseases, the one who shares in the life experiences of the afflicted, and according to the Latin translation of Isaiah 53:4 in the Vulgate, who, himself, is a leper. This ideological shift in Jesus' status proves necessary because of Matthew's definition of authority. The one who possesses true authority is the one who willingly stands in solidarity with those in need and provides a change for the better in their life situations (Matt. 11:2-6). Matthew challenges traditional Jewish leadership by suggesting that, through their ideological view of authority, they are misinterpreting the law that governed their society, so as to give priority to their social status at the expense of those whom they are to serve (Matt. 23:13-29).

Revisiting the Life Context

For those entrusted with guiding the average American citizen, and also a world citizen, in making critical life choices, Matthew's teaching on authority functions as "corrective lenses"—one of the roles of Scripture (see chapter 1, pp. 27-28). The authority with which they are entrusted is authority to empower people and to provide caring influence, not for oppressive domination and selfish prestige. Although we live in a world where the logic of the free market economy governs our existence, the goal of economic advancement must be subject to promoting and securing a quality life for our cocitizens. This is the charge and the mark of true authority. Matthew's teaching on authority also functions as an empowering Word (another role of Scripture) for citizens who feel increasingly powerless in this age of information and globalization. In ancient Palestine, it was the responsibility of a leper to secure healing for her or his physical symptoms and to initiate contact with a priest in order to gain legitimate reintegration into society. In Matthew 8:1-4, by approaching Jesus, the leper advances his cause and ultimately secures his cleansing. In a similar way, people in our contemporary world, strained by heavy burdens, hard to bear (see Matt. 11:28), have a responsibility to confront our leaders and to remind them of their obligation to stand in solidarity with those in crisis, to touch their lives, and to provide them with tools to live more fully. Matthew's teaching on authority presses each of us to move in the world as if *we are not on our own.*

4) Daniel Patte, Matthew in a Post-Holocaust European American Context

The Life Context

I was raised in a Protestant Huguenot family that participated in hiding Jewish people from the Nazis and their collaborators during World War II in occupied France. Thus, even as I was learning to read the Bible, as a child I was taught by my parents' deeds and words that Jews are members of God's chosen people and that anti-Judaism and anti-Semitism are in direct contradiction with the good news revealed in Christ Jesus, himself a Jew. After the Holocaust—the Shoah, the murder of six million Jews—interpretations of the New Testament that promote or condone anti-Judaism are scandalous.

Yet, still, many interpretations of Matthew implicitly or explicitly do so. These anti-Jewish readings are powerful and insidious because they are solidly grounded in the text of Matthew. For instance:

- In Matthew 3:7, John the Baptist rebukes Pharisees and Sadducees as a "brood of vipers" who follow a wrong teaching; a warning "to flee from the wrath to come";
- In Matthew 5:20, Jesus declares, "unless your righteousness exceeds that of the scribes and Pharisees, you will never enter the kingdom of heaven," a saying that can readily be understood as excluding scribes and Pharisees from the kingdom;
- In Matthew 21:23-43, to "the chief priests and the elders of the people," who asked Jesus, "By what authority are you doing these things?" Jesus responded by asking them about the authority of John the Baptist

and telling them the parable of the vineyard. He concludes: "Therefore I tell you, the kingdom of God will be taken away from you and given to a people that produces the fruits of the kingdom";

- In Matthew 23:1-39, after acknowledging the authority of "the scribes and Pharisees [who] sit on Moses' seat" (23:2) and their teaching (23:3), Jesus curses ("woe to you") the scribes and Pharisees and their hypocrisy;

- In Matthew 27:11-25, Pilate is aware that it was out of "jealousy" for Jesus' influence over the people that the chief priests and the elders "handed him over" (27:18), and therefore he wants to free Jesus. But at the instigation of the chief priests and elders (27:20), the people as a whole shouted, "Let him be crucified!" (27:23) and "His blood be on us and on our children!" (27:25).

It is easy to conclude from these and other verses that Matthew teaches Christians to view Jews—the scribes and Pharisees, all the Jewish people of Jesus' time, and their heirs today—as a cursed people, condemned by God. From this perspective, at minimum, Judaism is superseded by the gospel; the Jewish faith is hypocritical and needs to be replaced by the Christian faith; obtaining salvation and the kingdom requires abandoning and rejecting Judaism. This anti-Jewish teaching readily engenders anti-Jewish attitudes on the part of Christians, who then are prone to remain silent in the presence of anti-Semitic attitudes, and even to condone anti-Semitism. To our shame as Christians, this is what happened, especially in Europe and North America, during the Holocaust. It still happens.

The problem with this kind of interpretation is not a lack of textual evidence. The problem arises when one fails to acknowledge that, like any interpretation, this one is also based on the readers' interpretive choices. When these choices are ignored, it seems that there is no alternative but to view the Gospel as an anti-Jewish message. A redaction critical study of Matthew, such as that of Strecker (see chapter 2), readily grounds this anti-Jewish reading in the text. But this interpretation, like any other, involves choosing one dimension of the text as more significant than others. These textual choices also often correlate with theological and contextual choices sometimes even with abhorrent anti-Jewish theological and contextual choices. A practice of scriptural criticism that clarifies the interpretive choices of interpretations shows that anti-Jewish interpretations are not demanded by the text of Matthew. Other dimensions of Matthew do not carry such an anti-Jewish message and thus should be preferred.

Theological Issues Arising from This Life Context: The Gospel and Its Relationship to Jewish and Other Religious Teachings

What is the root problem of Christian anti-Judaism and anti-Semitism? Generally speaking, we can say that it is an inappropriate understanding (a wrong vision) of the relations between Jewish and Christian religious teachings. More specifically, the root problem is that the gospel (as a message) is envisioned as exclusivist, that is, as providing the exclusive access to God and God's will. From this perspective, the Christian faith requires believers to reject other religious teachings, including Jewish teachings. We need to raise the following theological question: Is Jesus teaching the gospel as proclaimed by Jesus (for example, Matt. 4:23) and his disciples (Matt. 10:7 and 28:19-20) exclusive or inclusive? Does it exclude other religious teachings and those who believe in them? In such a case the gospel is necessarily anti-Jewish. Or, is the gospel proclaimed by Jesus inclusive of other religious teachings? Does the kingdom proclaimed by Jesus include both insiders and outsiders, and thus people with different religious views and status? Does the kingdom defy the borders that make traditional religious communities exclusive? In this case, Jesus' rejection of Jewish authorities as presented by Matthew might be a rejection of their exclusivist claims.

In anti-Jewish readings of Matthew, Jesus' teaching and the Christian community presented by Matthew are understood in contrast with Jewish teachings and the synagogue. This theological stance is justified by viewing conflict as the most significant element in the interaction between Jesus and the Jewish authorities as presented by Matthew.

Alternatively, with Davies and Allison (see chapter 2), Christians can think of the conflicted interactions between Jesus and the Jewish authorities, and between Matthew's church and the synagogue, as family disputes among different branches within Judaism. These conflicts were not and could not be anti-Jewish. Rather, they raised the question: What is an appropriate Jewish religious teaching? Jesus, as a Jewish authority, offers answers that, at times, are in tension with those of other Jewish teachers and, at other times, are quite congruent with them.

One of the debated issues in Matthew and in the rest of Judaism at that time (for example, between the schools of Shammai and of Hillel) concerns the relationship between Jews and Gentiles, and thus between Jewish and other religious teachings. Should the people of God be closed upon itself in a truly positive relationship only with others who have entered the people of God? Or should the people of God be open and receptive to others, and if so, to what extent? In this second case, the question ultimately becomes: Are there sources of revelation outside of Judaism?

The choice of this theological issue as a focus for my interpretation of Matthew is appropriate. It is related to a contextual problem that concerns me as a post-Holocaust Christian: anti-Jewish and anti-Semitic interpretations.

Text Choices: Basic Convictions "in the Text"

In Matthew, the interrelation of Jesus' teaching with Jewish teachings and other religious teachings is a part of the structure of this Gospel that reflects basic convictions of the author.[22] To clarify these basic convictions, it is enough to ask regarding each pertinent passage: How does its ending reflect the transformation of the situation presented in its beginning? How is this transformation brought about?[23]

From the very beginning, Matthew surprises us. Repeatedly faithful characters in the story appeal to two kinds of religious teaching or revelation. Matthew 1:18-25 is the story of the naming of Jesus by Joseph. Without adoption by Joseph, a "son of David" (1:20), Jesus would not be recognized as "son of David" (1:1). At first, because Mary "was found to be with child" before they lived together, Joseph planned to dismiss her quietly. The reason for Joseph's decision is that he was "a righteous man," that is, he followed the Law of Moses. Joseph, we are told, was also "unwilling to expose her to public disgrace" (1:19), a sign of compassion in line with the prophetic teaching against a legalistic implementation of the Law. Thus, on the basis of the Jewish Scriptures alone, Joseph, a faithful, righteous Jew, was failing to do the right thing, namely keeping Mary with him and adopting Jesus. But he changes his mind and does the right thing (1:24-25) because of what he learned from an extrabiblical source, a dream in which an angel reveals to him that "the child conceived in [Mary] is from the Holy Spirit" (1:20). In sum, the teaching of the Jewish Scriptures is not enough. It needs to be complemented by an extrabiblical revelation, the dream, and angel.[24]

One could conclude from Matthew 1:18-25 that the Jewish Scriptures should be dismissed because they are superseded by another type of revelation. But the next story, Matthew 2:1-12, shows that this is the wrong conclusion. Seeing Jesus' star, an extrabiblical source, the Magi have learned about the birth of the "king of the Jews" and have been persuaded to go and pay him homage (2:2). Without this extrabiblical revelation, Herod, the chief priests, the scribes, and all of Jerusalem would not know about the birth or significance of Jesus. Conversely, without the biblical revelation (Mic. 5:2 and 2 Sam. 5:2) that the priests and the scribes have (Matt. 2:4-6), the Magi would not have known where to find Jesus in Bethlehem and would not have been able to pay him homage (2:11). In sum, both extrabiblical revelation (the star) and biblical revelation are needed. They complement each other.[25]

The reason for John the Baptist's reproof of the Pharisees and the Sadducees (Matt. 3:7-12) is that they rely exclusively on one kind of revelation. They say "we have Abraham as our ancestor" (3:9) and ignore the extrabiblical revelations—what God is doing in the present, including "[raising] up children to Abraham" from "these stones" (3:9), through John the Baptist (21:23-43) and through Jesus. The Jewish Scriptures are not closed as the Pharisees and the Sadducees presented by Matthew believe, but point beyond themselves to fulfillments in John's and in Jesus' ministries. This is what Matthew underscores by the formula quotations ("this was to fulfill what had been spoken by the Lord through the prophet," as in Matthew 1:22 and 2:5-6) and by numerous other allusions to the Scriptures. Jesus is both Son of God and King of the Jews. He is revelation beyond the Jewish Scriptures, only insofar as he submits himself to the will of God revealed in these Scriptures, as he does during his first temptation (4:1-11) and also during his last temptation, the passion (26:1–27:66).

Thus, Jesus underscores that he does not abolish the Law and the prophets, but "fulfills" them (Matt. 5:17; see 3:15). The biblical revelation points beyond itself to other manifestations of God's will and other interventions of God. The polemic against the scribes and Pharisees is not a rejection of their teaching. It includes the laws quoted in 5:21-48 and must be received and followed (23:2-3). The polemic against the scribes and the Pharisees is a rejection of their practice because it is narrowly limited to the scriptural revelation. Instead, Jesus' disciples are called to a righteousness that is "overabundant" (5:20, 46-47) because it is open to revelations of God's will beyond the Scriptures. Fulfilling the law means interpreting it in terms of other models of righteousness, those found among outsiders to the people of God. As the Magi followed the star, so Jesus' disciples should follow the tax collectors and Gentiles (5:46-47), as well as those who are blessed in the beatitudes (5:3-10), and even their own gut feelings about how they want to be treated by others (7:12). These are other sources of revelation that complement the Law and the prophets. Despite the imperfection of these people, Matthew offers their ways of life as models of righteousness for disciples to emulate in an overabundant way (loving not only one's friends but also one's enemies), just as disciples should fulfill in an overabundant way the Law and the prophets taught by the scribes and the Pharisees (5:17-20).[26]

This pattern of openness to other religious teachings is found throughout Matthew. One finds it, for example, in the story of the Canaanite woman (Matt. 15:22-28), a woman who through her Gentile wisdom and faith reveals to Jesus a new dimension of his ministry. It is also in Matthew 28:16-20 as the Great Commission is read as the conclusion of the passion story (Matt. 26–28). It is only by the passion that the male followers of Jesus are transformed into full-fledged disciples ready to go in mission. According to Matthew, these disciples have not yet participated in mission (despite being sent in Matthew 10:5-42, they never go). In Matthew 26, they are self-assured; they believe they have all the necessary knowledge, motivation, and strength to follow Jesus (as they affirm with Peter, in 26:31-35). As followers of Jesus throughout his ministry, did they know they had received from him all the revealed knowledge they needed? But, after denying and abandoning Jesus, they lost this self-assurance. So when they met the resurrected Christ, "they worshiped him; but they doubted" (28:17, my more literal translation). Their doubt, and therefore their awareness that they must be open to receive new teachings, is an inclusive attitude. Their recognizing that what they have is not sufficient shows that they are at last ready to carry out their mission. Their mission must therefore be as open as Jesus' ministry was. It is a mission that is open to the sources of revelation found among the Gentiles (or nations)—their dreams, visions of angels, stars, and the like—while keeping its Jewish grounding in the Law and the prophets. The Jewish Scriptures are to be fulfilled, not abolished.

Revisiting the Life Context

This interpretation can be supported by more textual evidence.[27] Its theological conclusions are clear. The gospel of Jesus Christ remains quite distinct from Judaism and other religions through its proclamation of the kingdom (Matt. 10:7). Yet its integrity is maintained only by the constant affirmation of the validity of Jewish teachings, seen as complementary with other religious teachings. From the perspective of this interpretation, there is no hesitation: Abhorrent anti-Jewish interpretations of the Gospel of Matthew—though plausible—are in direct contradiction to the gospel of Jesus Christ. Such interpretations should and can be pushed aside to make room for other, inclusive interpretations, such as the one above.

B) Holding the Second Roundtable Discussion
on Matthew 1–28

Hold the second roundtable discussion, under the leadership of a member facilitator, as usual. Keep in mind that the facilitator's goal is to help the members of the group identify and refine their contextual, theological, and textual choices. Thus, each of the four interpretations presented above should be discussed in the process of comparing their interpretive choices with those of the participants. Each participant should also identify which of these four interpretations is closer to his or hers—a good basis to refine one's interpretation. Thus, each participant should come to the roundtable after completing the following chart. This requires you to identify and summarize the contextual, theological, and textual choices of each of the four above interpretations.

C) Sharing Results

Under the leadership of a member scribe, share the results of the second roundtable. In preparation for the third roundtable, it is particularly helpful for you to be aware if your interpretation is somewhat similar to one of the four published ones.

Interpreters' Contextual Choices	Revelation E. Velunta	Justin Ukpong	Monya A. Stubbs	Daniel Patte	Your Interpretation
1) Problem in the Interpreters' Life Context (see chap. 1, pp. 29-32)	1)	1)	1)	1)	1)
2) Root Problem (see chap. 1, pp. 29-32)	2)	2)	2)	2)	2)

Interpreters' Theological Choices	Revelation E. Velunta	Justin Ukpong	Monya A. Stubbs	Daniel Patte	Your Interpretation
1) Role of the Text as Scripture (see chap. 1, pp. 27-28)	1)	1)	1)	1)	1)
2) Theological Concepts	2)	2)	2)	2)	2)

Interpreters' Textual Choices	Revelation E. Velunta	Justin Ukpong	Monya A. Stubbs	Daniel Patte	Your Interpretation
1) Most Significant Textual Features (see chap. 2, pp. 54-57)	1)	1)	1)	1)	1)
2) Methods (see chap. 2, pp. 54-57)	2)	2)	2)	2)	2)

III—Third Roundtable Discussion on Matthew 1–28

Four different interpretations are presented above. Each one is appropriately based on a significant aspect of the Gospel of Matthew. Each one is appropriately focused on certain theological concepts. Which one is "the best" reading? Which one is "the worst"? In order to assess the relative values of these four different interpretations, in a debate format, the Bible study group should first select a particular life context. Since each of us has emphasized a particular context, it is the turn of the Bible study group to choose a context!

When this concrete situation is chosen, four participants should make a case for one of these interpretations as offering the best and one as offering the worst teaching for believers in this situation. Remember the twofold criterion for assessing the relative value of interpretations and their effects on believers and their neighbors: love of God and love of neighbors.

Notes

1. The Gospel of Matthew is a narrative discourse constructed and framed by Roman imperial occupation. In other words, it is a story that has a message for people in this imperialistic situation.

2. See Leela Gandhi, *Postcolonial Theory* (New York: Columbia University Press, 1998), 32.

3. Quoted in Daniel B. Schirmer and Stephen Rosskamm Shalom, eds., *The Philippines Reader: A History of Colonialism, Neocolonialism, Dictatorship, and Resistance* (Boston: South End Press, 1987), 12.

4. UNAIDS website, "Report on the Global HIV/AIDS Epidemic June 2000," http://www.unaids.org.in/

5. Bruce J. Malina and Richard L. Rohrbaugh, *Social Science Commentary on the Synoptic Gospels* (Minneapolis: Fortress Press, 1992), 71. Warren Carter, *Matthew and the Margins: A Sociopolitical and Religious Reading* (Maryknoll, N.Y.: Orbis Books, 2000), 124-25.

6. Carter, *Matthew and the Margins*, 124-25.

7. See T. R. France, *Matthew: Tyndale New Testament Commentaries* (Grand Rapids: Eerdmans, 1985), 94-95.

8. Segundo Galilea, *The Beatitudes: To Evangelize as Jesus Did* (Maryknoll, N.Y.: Orbis Books, 1984), 13.

9. Carter, *Matthew and the Margins*, 131-32.

10. William R. Herzog II, *Jesus, Justice, and the Reign of God: A Ministry of Liberation* (Louisville, Ky.: Westminster John Knox Press, 2000), 105-8.

11. Bruce Malina, *The Social World of Jesus and the Gospels* (London: Routledge, 1996), 45.

12. The 28 January 2002 issue of *Time* includes the following articles: "You're on Your Own: The Enron Lesson in Making Critical Decisions, Consumers Are at Sea" and "Your Money: Old Safety Nets Are Gone. Here's What to Do," both by Daniel Kadlec; "Health: Where to Get Help in a Constantly Changing System" by

Michael Lemonick; and "Getting Connected: How to Untangle All Those Offers" by Lev Grossman.

13. Kadlec, "You're on Your Own," 24.

14. Ibid.

15. Ibid.

16. Ibid., 25.

17. This issue becomes clear when Matthew is read from an ideological perspective (see below, the discussion of key passages).

18. Louis Althusser, *Essays on Ideology* (London: Verso, 1984), 36.

19. Josephus, *Jewish Antiquities III,* 266-70.

20. Josephus, *Against Apion I,* 281. Hannah K. Harrington, *The Impurity Systems of Qumran and the Rabbis Biblical Foundations.* SBL Dissertation Series 143 (Atlanta: Scholars Press, 1993), 80.

21. Ched Myers, *Building the Strong Man: A Political Reading of Mark's Story of Jesus* (Maryknoll, N.Y.: Orbis Books, 1997), 146.

22. Daniel Patte, *The Gospel According to Matthew* (Philadelphia: Fortress Press, 1987), 1-15.

23. See the place of structural methods in the chart "Bible Study Methods and the Textual Features They Emphasize" on pages 54-57.

24. Patte, *Gospel According to Matthew,* 16-28.

25. Ibid., 32-36.

26. Ibid., 60-105. See also Daniel Patte, *Discipleship According to the Sermon on the Mount: Four Legitimate Readings, Four Plausible Views of Discipleship, and Their Relative Values* (Harrisburg, Pa.: Trinity Press International, 1986), 198-260 and 312-50; and *The Challenge of Discipleship: A Critical Study of the Sermon on the Mount as Scripture* (Harrisburg, Pa.: Trinity Press International, 1999), 162-76.

27. See Patte, *Gospel According to Matthew, Discipleship According to the Sermon on the Mount,* and *Challenge of Discipleship.*

Works Consulted

Abesamis, Carlos. *A Third Look at Jesus*. Quezon City, Philippines: Claretian Publications, 1999.

Althusser, Louis. *Essays on Ideology*. London: Verso, 1984.

Carter, Warren. *Matthew and the Margins: A Sociopolitical and Religious Reading*. Maryknoll, N.Y.: Orbis Books, 2000.

Constantino, Renato. *Neocolonial Identity and Counter-consciousness: Essays on Cultural Decolonization*. White Plains, N.Y.: M. E. Sharpe, 1978.

Davies, W. D. and Dale C. Allison Jr. *Critical and Exegetical Commentary on the Gospel According to St. Matthew*, 3 vols. T & T Clark, 1988.

De La Torre, Edicio. "The Philippines: A Situationer." In *Those Who Would Give Light Must Endure Burning*. Ed. Romeo M. Bautista and Samuel Amirtham. Quezon City, Philippines: National Council of Churches in the Philippines, 1977.

Dube, Musa W. *Postcolonial Feminist Interpretation of the Bible*. St. Louis, Mo.: Chalice Press, 2000.

Fanon, Franz. *The Wretched of the Earth*. Trans. Constance Farrington. New York: Grove Weidenfeld, 1968.

France, T. R. *Matthew: Tyndale New Testament Commentaries*. Grand Rapids, Mich.: Eerdmans, 1985.

Freire, Paulo. *Pedagogy of the Oppressed*. Trans. Myra Bergman Ramos. New York: Herder and Herder, 1970.

Fernandez, Eleazar S. *Toward a Theology of Struggle*. Maryknoll, N.Y.: Orbis Books, 1994.

Galilea, Segundo. *The Beatitudes: To Evangelize as Jesus Did*. Maryknoll, N.Y.: Orbis Books, 1984.

Harrington, Hannah K. *The Impurity Systems of Qumran and the Rabbis: Biblical Foundation*. SBL Dissertation Series 143. Atlanta: Scholars Press, 1993.

Herzog, William R., II. *Jesus, Justice, and the Reign of God: A Ministry of Liberation*. Louisville, Ky.: Westminster John Knox Press, 2000.

Ileto, Reynaldo Clemeña. *Pasyon and Revolution: Popular Movements in the Philippines, 1840–1910*. Quezon City, Philippines: Ateneo de Manila University Press, 1979.

Leela Gandhi. *Postcolonial Theory: A Critical Introduction*. New York: Columbia University Press, 1998.

Malina, Bruce J. *The Social World of Jesus and the Gospels*. New York: Routledge, 1996.

Malina, Bruce J., and Richard L. Rohrbaugh. *Social Science Commentary on the Synoptic Gospels*. Minneapolis: Fortress Press, 1992.

Myers, Ched. *Binding the Strong Man: A Political Reading of Mark's Story of Jesus*. Maryknoll, N.Y.: Orbis Books, 1988.

Overman, J. Andrew. *Church and Community in Crisis: The Gospel According to Matthew*. Valley Forge, Pa.: Trinity Press International, 1996.

Patte, Daniel, 1987. *The Gospel According to Matthew: A Structural Commentary on Matthew's Faith*. Philadelphia: Fortress Press; third reprint, Valley Forge, Pa.: Trinity Press International, 1996.

———. *Discipleship According to the Sermon on the Mount: Four Legitimate Readings, Four Plausible Views of Discipleship, and Their Relative Values*. Valley Forge, Pa.: Trinity Press International, 1996.

———. *The Challenge of Discipleship: A Critical Study of the Sermon on the Mount as Scripture*. Harrisburg, Pa.: Trinity Press International, 1999.

Powell, Mark Allan. *Chasing the Eastern Star: Adventures in Reader-Response Criticism*. Louisville, Ky.: Westminster John Knox Press, 2001.

Schirmer, Daniel. "The Conception and Gestation of a Neocolony." *The Journal of Contemporary Asia* 5. no. 1 (1975): 43-44.

Senior, Donald. *The Gospel of Matthew*. Nashville: Abingdon Press, 1997.

"Report on the Global HIV/AIDS Epidemic June 2000." UNAIDS website.

Velunta, Revelation. "The Ho Pais Mou of Matthew 8:5-13: Contesting the Interpretations in the Name of Present-day Paides." *Bulletin for Contextual Theology* 7 no. 2. (June 2000): 25-32.

Waetjen, Herman C. *A Reordering of Power: A Sociopolitical Reading of Mark's Gospel*. Minneapolis: Fortress Press, 1989.